DISCIPLESHIP 1
THE FUNDAMENTALS OF CHRISTIANITY
A BEGINNING STUDY IN CHRISTIAN DISCIPLESHIP

Copyright © 2016 by Charlie Webster

ISBN 978-0-9894290-3-0

Catalog as Religion - Practical Theology - Practical Religion – The Christian Life as Religion - Christian Experience, Practice, and Life (Dewey Decimal 248).

For further information on this book or the author, visit

www.NewCenturyMinistries.com

ACKNOWLEDGEMENT & NOTES

I'm deeply indebted to college professors, Christian leaders (professional and non-professional), and various individuals among my family and friends who've contributed to my understanding of the Bible and my ability to write this book. I especially thank those who offered me the one thing I value most—good criticism that forced me to think through what I was saying from different perspectives. And I cannot overstate how important the advice and support of Karen, my wife, has been in this process. It's to her that I dedicate this effort.

NOTE TO A GROUP STUDY LEADER*: There's a Leader's Guide in Appendix A. Please go over that material carefully before attempting to lead a group in this study; then review it at regular times after beginning the study. And please understand that this study requires serious time for prayer and study on the part of the leader. Neglect of either the prayer time or the study time will seriously affect the results of the study.*

After each section there are Points to Consider. Many of these start with the words, "Seriously consider..." If you're leading a study group, these are good discussion items. However, please read the Leader's Guide and understand how to get group discussion going before trying to use these discussion points. If nothing else, learn the 60 second rule and use it.

Some sections are longer than others. Some may take less than your normal time for the group, and others may take more. Rather than going over the normal time limit, consider continuing the discussion the next time you get together. If you have extra time, consider reviewing previous sections or discuss application of the things learned.

NOTE TO THE STUDY PARTICIPANT*: This study is for those who have genuinely made a discipleship commitment to follow Jesus. This is a very serious commitment, the most serious commitment in this world, and it shouldn't be approached lightly. This is for those who want a better understanding of what Christianity is all about, a stronger faith in and relationship with God, and a better hope for now and for eternity. If you're not a Christian, you may find this study helpful in considering the claims of Christianity, but this study is primarily meant to encourage and inspire Christians.*

NOTE TO AN INDIVIDUAL READER*: This study is primarily for a small group environment where the ideas presented can be discussed by the group. Throughout the study there are suggestions of "Points to Consider" that are meant to be discussion areas. Obviously, most individual readers will not carry on those discussions, but I encourage you to seriously consider these topics. And if you find the material stimulating, I encourage you to seek a few friends or acquaintances who would share this study with you. This is a study you can do repeatedly and still gain from it. I wrote it, edited it, and I've taught this material repeatedly, and I'm still learning from it.*

NOTE ON GOSPEL REFERENCES*: This study has several notes at the end of each section of the study. Many of these notes simply tell where something in the study can be found in the Bible. For those notes that point to the Gospels (Matthew, Mark, Luke, and John), there are at least two references given for each passage. The first reference is to the passage in* Good News! The Life and Teaching of Jesus, *a translation that combines everything from all four Gospels into a single account. This is followed by reference to one or more passages in the individual Gospels where the same information can be found. If you have a copy of* Good News! The Life and Teaching of Jesus, *you will probably find it easier to refer to the passage in that translation. If you don't have a copy of that translation, use any other translation you like. All quotations from the Gospels in this study are from* Good News! The Life and Teaching of Jesus.

TABLE OF CONTENTS

CHRISTIANITY 100 – DISCIPLESHIP OVERVIEW

NOT YOUR NORMAL CONCEPTS

If you expect this study to be a re-affirmation of the traditions you've accepted since childhood, you've got the wrong idea. One of Satan's favorite tactics is to take our Christian traditions and gently, over time, move those traditions away from what Jesus actually taught, until, in many cases, our traditions actually work against the Lord. In this study, we're going to focus on what the Bible really does teach us about what Jesus wants and expects—and even demands—from his followers in three of the most fundamental areas. We'll find that there's extreme eternal danger in practicing traditions without checking to make sure that those traditions are what the Lord would want.

So where are we going in this study? What does it take to be a disciple and why should you take the trouble and time to be one? Can't you be saved without being a serious disciple? If you believe in God and Jesus and you go to church, isn't that more than enough? These are important questions for this generation, and they need some serious answers, because being a real disciple does require investing your time and effort. And unfortunately, the answers being given by most Christian organizations today are not consistent with the biblical message.

A Christian is a disciple of Jesus, one who's accepted Jesus as Lord over every aspect of his or her life. That's the reality. That's the biblical message over and over. And that's the message that's too often being neglected. That doesn't mean that Christians are perfect or that they are even all that good at implementing their discipleship, but Christianity is a serious commitment to growth in serving Jesus in every area of life[1].

So what does that commitment involve? First, it's not about rituals, ceremonies, or incantations. It's not about clergy and it's not about the music. It's not about buildings. All of these things are just tools, and if we think of these in any other way, we miss the point.

Actually, Christianity is about life itself, and the heart and soul of Christianity is about Christian love. Unfortunately, many, many Christians don't know what that is, and we'll start our study focusing on that aspect of Christianity. For right now it's enough to say that Christian love is very different from what we normally think of as love. It looks for the needs of others and does what it can to meet those needs. For real Christians, their Christianity is their life focused on Christian love, because that's who God is.

But why would you want to make such a commitment to Jesus? This study will show you why, but let's start with the bottom line: What if you were given access to a real fountain of youth that would keep you young and healthy as long as you wanted—even healing any injury or disease of any severity? And what if, in conjunction with that youth and health, someone gave you something to do that you would just love doing—something that you'd see as exciting and very rewarding? Beyond that, what if, as you did your work, all the people around you were eager to help you succeed and find joy in the work you do as well as in your vacations? And to top it all off, suppose you were doing this in the most beautiful location you can imagine, with time for recreation and fun in a wide variety of wonderful places? What would you be willing to do or go through in order to gain that?

These are important matters, because, as we'll see in this study, that's exactly what God's promised to anyone who'll join his side in this world and get serious about learning to live his way. In fact, the reward is even better than that! But we'll get to that later.

In recent years there's been a popular teaching that the ultimate purpose of a Christian's life is to bring glory to God. Christians' lives are to bring glory to God, but that's not the purpose for our lives. That teaching implies that God created billions of people to see how many would tell him what a good God he really is. That makes God an egotistical monster. That would mean that God created all these people just to tell him how wonderful he is, and that he did this when he knew that most of them wouldn't cooperate. He even knew that the ones who did cooperate would have to be saved at the cost of the cross. That certainly isn't consistent with a God who is love of any sort. And that makes God look like he has a raging inferiority complex and a serious need for reassurance.

It's not that God doesn't want our praise, but he only wants it when it's sincere, when it's given because we're so excited about the good things he's doing in our lives and the good things he's promised us yet to come that we can't keep quiet. Our primary purpose in this life isn't to praise God; it's to get ready for the wonderful and

---

[1] See Good News 9:34-69 (Matthew 5:21-48).

exciting eternity God's preparing for us. God wants our lives to bring glory to him, not because he has an inferiority complex, but because this will draw more people to him and to the wonderful eternity he's planned. God is love. He's got wonderful things in store for us. But we can't even get into his eternity if we don't learn some of the most important lessons he's teaching us in this world. And that's what this study of discipleship is all about. We'll look at the three most fundamental principles of Christianity: Christian love, saving faith, and heavenly hope; and we'll find that too many of the traditional ideas that Christians hold about these principles are not what Jesus taught.

If this doesn't sound like the Christianity you've heard about, that's not too surprising. Almost every branch and group of Christians has been distracted by traditions and doctrines instead of the life Jesus came to offer. Jesus said that his message is good news. If the message we carry isn't the best news ever, we can be sure it's not the message Jesus brought.

Points to Consider:
1. Seriously consider the ideas in this section. In what ways are these ideas similar to the ideas you had of Christianity? Be specific.
2. In what ways do these ideas seem different from the ideas you had of Christianity? Be specific.
3. Focus on the popular idea that the ultimate purpose of Christians is to glorify God. Seriously consider what this would say about God. What are your thoughts about people who constantly want others to talk about how good they are?

GETTING OFF COURSE

I heard the pilot's voice say, "Do you see anything you recognize down there?" I was in a small commuter plane going from Little Rock to Memphis. I was sitting in the first seat behind the cockpit, and there was only a curtain between my seat and the cockpit. What I was hearing was a discussion between the pilot and the co-pilot. This was before GPS, and that wasn't the most comforting conversation to hear.

If you don't have GPS or some form of radio navigation, and you can't spot a landmark, you can get way off course flying an airplane. In the same way, if we don't have reliable guidance, we can get way off course in our Christianity. God has provided two sources of guidance—the Bible and his Holy Spirit—but if we don't pay close attention to that guidance, we're sure to get off course.

And if an airplane gets into a storm, it's possible for the pilots to lose their navigation instrumentation and for the airplane to be blown far off course. In the same way, the storms of this life can get us far off course and cause us to lose contact with the navigation that God is providing. Those storms do come—Satan makes sure of that—and if we lose focus in the storms, it can be very hard to get back on course. It's as if the aircraft is flying very well, and feels very comfortable and safe, but we're going the wrong way. To make matters worse, Satan sends his servants to tell us that we're not off course, and he often dresses them up to look like Christians.

Jesus once said, "Nobody's dumb enough to put a patch of new, unshrunk wool on an older woolen garment. If you do that, the patch shrinks the first time it's washed and pulls at the old garment, making the tear worse than ever. In the same way, people know better than to put new wine into wineskins that have become brittle with age. If they do that, when the wine ferments it expands breaking the wineskin and spilling the wine. New wine has to be put into new skins so that both will go through the fermentation process safely. But once folks have had the old wine, they won't soon want to change. They think the old's better[2]."

The New Testament is the map for Christians, but that was written almost 2,000 years ago. Today, we need help understanding that map. We need a reliable translation in English that uses words and phrases that are familiar enough to us to allow us to make sense of the message. In addition, many of the customs and cultural norms of Bible times are no longer familiar to us, so we need some background information to help us understand how things described in the Bible should be understood today.

It's not that the Bible's wrong, it's just that we need to understand it in a way that communicates the same things to us that it communicated to those who first read it. And we need faithful people who'll help us as we study the Bible and try to apply its lessons. This book and its companion (Good News: The Life and Teachings of

---

[2] See Good News 16:55-57 (Matthew 9:16-17; Mark 2:22-23; Luke 5:36-39).

Jesus) are meant to help in these areas. But most of all we need God's Holy Spirit to guide us in our understanding. He's with us to help, but we need to seek his help and listen carefully for his guidance.

Points to Consider:
1. Seriously consider any specific situations that you or members of the group know about where traditions have caused Christians to get off course. As an example, you may want to look up information about Galileo.
2. Think about a time when you had bad directions to some destination you were trying to reach. Seriously consider the difficulty of getting back on course when you've got bad directions. In what situations can Christians get wrong directions?
3. Seriously consider ways for Christians to detect wrong directions. What might Satan do to try to keep us from detecting that we're off course?
4. Seriously consider ways for us as Christians to be sure we're making progress in the right direction.

THE BIBLE VERSUS TRADITION

Most of us as Christians claim the Bible as our guide. We advertise that we're all about implementing the pattern of Christianity approved in the New Testament, modified only to make exactly the same message communicate well to this generation. But is that really the truth?

Too often we prefer our comfortable traditions to serious Christianity, but that's a very dangerous path. During his earthly ministry, there was no one Jesus condemned more soundly than the Pharisees, and he condemned them for exactly this problem of clinging to tradition instead of paying attention to God's voice. Often our traditions are the result of Satan's gentle pressures to send us in a wrong direction.

So at this point we come back to where we started. Getting to know real Christianity requires some effort. That's the first step in discipleship—learning what Christianity's all about. And right now you need to realize that if you're not willing to make some serious changes in your life to gain what God has to offer, you'd be wasting your time to participate in this study. What God offers is valuable beyond imagination, and it's far more than just a "Get-Out-of-Hell-Free" card, but there's a price. You need to count the cost before you even start[3].

Just so we get off to a good start, Christianity is about God's plan, and God's plan is about saving faith, eternal hope, and Christian love. What we'll find is that there's no real mystery here—the message of Christianity runs through the Bible like a freight train. The only problem is the misinformation that gets us going wrong directions, and in these studies, we'll find a lot of that. If it weren't for the misinformation, these studies wouldn't be so necessary. These studies will just keep pointing you back to the Bible and to what makes sense from God's perspective as presented in the Bible. Once you get God's message, you'll find the right way to your destination.

Points to Consider:
1. Seriously consider what pictures come to your mind when you think of God's Holy Spirit being turned loose in a person's life. Is this something good or bad? Is it possible you have a wrong idea of what it means for God's Holy Spirit to be turned loose in a person's life?
2. Seriously consider your reaction to the idea that Christianity is about saving faith, eternal hope, and Christian love. What is your initial reaction to this? Is there something you think should be added to or taken away from that list?
3. Seriously consider how much you're willing to change in order to get what God has to offer.

Summary Questions:
1. Did this section help you in any way, and if so, how? Be specific.

2. What do you see as the most important point or points of this section when it comes to Christians being motivated?

---

[3] See Good News 35:33-36 (Luke 14:28-33).

3. Jot down a note or two about anything you learned new in studying this section or anything you understood better because of studying this section.

CHRISTIANITY 101-A – THE GOOD NEWS OF CHRISTIAN LOVE - PART 1

In every way, treat people the way you wish they'd treat you.
That's the point of everything God ever told you in the Law of
Moses and the writings of the prophets[1].

In writing to the Christians in Corinth Paul said, "Now we have these three enduring factors: faith, hope, and caring love; but the greatest of these is caring love[2]." That kind of love certainly is the first key principle of Christianity. After all, God is that kind of love[3]. It may seem like stating the obvious to say that this is good news, but in fact it can be both very good news and very bad news. Properly understood, Christian love provides both the carrot and the stick of motivation—both motivation to want to be a Christian and motivation to fear not being a Christian. In the two parts of this session we'll look at the good news aspect of Christian love. In the two parts of the next session we'll look at the bad news of what happens when we don't practice Christian love. Before we're through with this study, we'll find that Christian love is very good news indeed. We'll consider several aspects of that good news in this session.

GOOD NEWS!

The good news of the gospel is truly astonishing good news. But the sad fact is that most Christians, when they really grasp how good the news is, will be astonished themselves—they've never really grasped what's truly their birthright. I hope and believe that each person who shares in this study will come to see the good news of the gospel as more awesome and wonderful than he or she had ever realized. For anyone who understands this good news, Christianity should represent the most exciting, wonderful, and thrilling aspect of life.

CHRISTIAN LOVE[4] DEFINED

A lot of professional Christian leaders have delivered a lot of sermons about Christian love, in part because in English the word "love" has so many variations of meaning, most of which don't apply to Christian love. What I plan to do here is give a definition that's both biblical and practical. If it's biblical without affecting how we live, it's not practical. Christianity must affect how we live or it's worthless. In fact, we'll find the definition given in this section is a definition given first by Jesus, and later by his followers.

Many Christians have at least heard of the Greek word, "*agape*" (pronounced ah-GAH-pay) as the word Jesus used for Christian love. This word was used frequently in the Jewish sacred writings (our Old Testament) when those writings were translated into Greek, giving Jesus exactly the background he needed to emphasize his definition. However, it was a word that wasn't well defined or frequently used in secular Greek writings. Jesus took that word, defined it in his own way, and made that concept the core of his message.

In the Bible, 1Corinthians 13 is known as the love chapter—a passage the apostle Paul wrote to describe Christian love. We'll get to that, but I want to start with a story Jesus told to provide his description of Christian love:

> An expert in Jewish laws stood up in the crowd to test Jesus. "Teacher," he asked, "what should I do to gain eternal life?"
> "What does it say in the Law of Moses?" Jesus asked. "How do you understand what it says?"

---

[1] Good News 11:15 (Matthew 7:12; Luke 6:31).
[2] 1Corinthians 13:13 (The "caring love" here is Christian love, as explained below).
[3] See 1John 4:8, 16.
[4] The word used in the New Testament for Christian love was a rarely used word before Jesus' ministry. Jesus took this word and defined it, making it the very core of God's dealings with humanity. While the biblical text doesn't use the term "Christian love," wherever the word "*agape*" appears in the Greek text, we can be sure the meaning is Christian love as Jesus defined it.

"'You shall care for Jehovah your God with all your heart, with all your soul, with all your strength, and with all your mind[5],'" the lawyer responded, "and 'you shall care for your neighbor as you care for yourself[6].'"

"Well," said Jesus, "you've got the right answers. Do that and you'll have eternal life."

Wanting to show off how correct he was, the lawyer asked Jesus, "And just who is my neighbor?"

"There was a Jewish man[7]," Jesus responded, "who was traveling on the road down from Jerusalem to Jericho[8]. On this trip, he was attacked by thieves who stripped off his clothing, beat him, and then ran off leaving him for dead. As it happened, the next man to come down that road was a Jewish priest[9], but when he saw the man who'd been robbed, he moved over to the far side of the road and just kept going. Not long after that a Levite[10] came by and looked at the man, but then he did exactly what the priest had done.

"Then a Samaritan who was traveling that way came to the place where the man lay bleeding. When he saw the man, his heart went out to this Jew[11]. He went to the man's side and started caring for him, bandaging his wounds and pouring on oil and wine to prevent infection. Then he set the man on his own animal and brought him to a traveler's inn where he continued to care for him.

"The next day, before he left the inn, the Samaritan gave $160[12] to the man in charge of the inn and told him, 'Take care of that fellow. If you have to spend more than this, I'll cover the bill next time I come through here.' So now," Jesus asked, "Which of these three men was a neighbor to the one who was attacked by thieves?"

"The one who cared for him[13]," answered the lawyer.

"Go and demonstrate that kind of caring love[14]," Jesus concluded[15].

Given this illustration of Christian love from Jesus, what can we say about the definition of this kind of love? I'll offer five suggestions—you may have others:

1. Christian love chooses to forgive—setting aside retribution as God's job, not a job for any human. Most Jews treated Samaritans as the scum of the earth. A Jew would avoid any contact with a Samaritan, and some Jewish teachers held that it would be wrong to help a Samaritan woman in childbirth, because this simply helped bring another Samaritan into the world. But the Samaritan in Jesus' story was able to turn retribution over to God, forgiving anything this particular Jew might or might not have done, and caring for him as simply a man in need.

2. Christian love chooses to care about the needs of others, just as this Samaritan man saw the need of a wounded Jew and chose to care. His heart went out to this man in need. A priest and a Levite had made their choices to ignore the man's need. Though "religious leaders," they didn't want to get involved and risk being defiled by a dead body.

---

[5] Deuteronomy 6:5.

[6] Leviticus 19:18.

[7] The Bible only says a man, but the fact that he was Jewish is clearly implied and necessary for the story.

[8] This was a steep and winding mountain road from Jerusalem in the mountains to Jericho in a very deep valley.

[9] The Bible doesn't specifically say "Jewish," but the fact that he was Jewish is clearly implied and necessary for the story.

[10] Members of the Levite tribe were responsible for various duties at the temple. Among the Israelites, all Levites were considered especially dedicated to God's service.

[11] This story is Jesus' definition of Christian love, and it starts with forgiveness when a Samaritan, whose people had been abused, maligned, and mistreated by Jews for centuries, decided to turn retribution over to God and care for this suffering Jew.

[12] Literally, "two denarii...," but this would be about equal to 160 American dollars in about 2010.

[13] This lawyer couldn't even bring himself to say "Samaritan."

[14] The word here is for the caring love that is Christian love.

[15] Good News 22:21-35 (Luke 10:25-37).

3. Christian love chooses to be unselfish. From his conversation with an innkeeper, we can see that this Samaritan was a businessman who traveled this road regularly, but he put his own interests and his business aside to deal with the needs of this wounded Jew.
4. Christian love chooses to be generous. Even after using his own oil, his own wine, his own cloth, his own time, and his own beast of burden, this Samaritan was ready to give the innkeeper enough money to provide for this stranger's needs until he might be well enough to travel on his own.
5. Christian love chooses to be active. This Samaritan man didn't just wish the man well as he passed by or offer to send help when he reached the next community. He didn't have a servant deal with the man's wounds. He cleaned the wounds as best he could. He bandaged the wounds. He put the man on his animal. He got his hands dirty and bloody. He got involved.

Notice that each of these characteristics is a choice. Christian love isn't an emotional reaction over which we have no control. Christian love is a choice (or a series of choices) that we make. You can't have a real emotional love for someone you despise, but you can choose to practice Christian love toward such a person, and in this passage we see that this is the real point of all God's commandments. Even using the English word "love" is a problem, because when we think of love we normally think of something that involves emotion or sex, but, although Christian love can bring about an emotional bond, Christian love is not an emotion at all—it's a choice. FROM THIS POINT ON IN THIS STUDY, WE'LL USE THE WORDS "CARING LOVE" FOR THIS LOVE.

Before we take the next step in this study, just think for a moment what this world would be like if everyone practiced this kind of forgiving, caring, unselfish, generous, and active love. What could be more heavenly? This wouldn't just mean a total absence of war and strife and crime of any sort, it would mean everyone around us would always be concerned to meet our needs and do what's best for us—and we'd feel the same about them. So God's commandments are getting us ready for what heaven must be. This is extremely important, and we'll come back to this point over and over.

Now let's consider Paul's words about this caring love:

> Caring love is willing to bear up for long periods of suffering. Caring love is kind. Caring love doesn't envy what others have. Caring love doesn't show off, isn't proud of what it's done. Caring love doesn't behave rudely. Caring love isn't selfish or easily provoked. Caring love doesn't go around looking for the evil in others. Indeed, caring love finds no pleasure in doing wrong. Rather, caring love finds pleasure in the truth. Caring love is ready to bear whatever's necessary, trusting in God regardless of circumstances, staying focused on our hope no matter what, and enduring whatever may come. Caring love never fails[16].

Paul's words help clarify and strengthen what Jesus taught, but the five points listed above from Jesus' story that we call "The Good Samaritan" form the foundation for everything Paul said. And it all starts with really caring about the needs of others—keeping our eyes open and our ears alert to be aware of those needs.

If you wonder why this kind of love is so important to God, we'll look at several reasons next.

Points to Consider:
1. Seriously consider how you agree or disagree with the concept that Jesus' story about a Samaritan helping a dying Jew is Jesus' definition of caring love.
2. Seriously consider each of the five points suggested as part of Jesus' definition of caring love. For each of these individually, do you agree or disagree about it being an intentional part of Jesus' definition of caring love?
3. Seriously consider what other aspects of caring love are brought out in Paul's description. Do you see anything in Paul's words that isn't implied in the story Jesus told?
4. Seriously consider any problems related to practicing this kind of caring "love" in our world today. What are some of the problems you see?

---

[16] 1Corinthians 13:4-8.

5. Seriously consider any benefits or advantages related to practicing this kind of "love" in our world today. What benefits or advantages do you see?
6. Seriously consider the idea of caring love as a choice (or a set of choices) as compared to other concepts of love. Does this seem consistent with Jesus' story?

CARING LOVE – PREPARATION FOR HEAVEN

While heaven will be beautiful and there'll be a lot of good things about heaven (more about this in Christianity 103 later in this study), the one thing more than any other that'll make heaven a paradise is caring love. Since we'll address heaven in Christianity 103, at this point we'll limit our discussion of this topic—but can you imagine living in a place where everyone you meet will care about you and want to help your life be the best it can be? No one to fear; no one to doubt—whatever a person in heaven does or says, you'll know it was with the very best of intentions. Now, while there's a lot more to what makes heaven wonderful, "ain't-a that good news!!!" Just imagine how wonderful that would be!

Points to Consider:
1. Seriously consider the concept that the commandments to practice caring love are actually getting us ready for heaven. Does that seem consistent with a God who is love? Does that seem like a good thing to you?
2. Seriously consider the concept that obeying the commandments to practice caring love would make the earth more like heaven. Does that seem like something that a God who is love would want?
3. Seriously consider how this might or might not be good news. Does it seem like good news to you? Does it seem like news you'd want to share with others?

CARING LOVE – GOD'S TOOL FOR EVANGELISM

In his first general letter the apostle Peter wrote to Christians telling them to always be ready to give an answer to anyone who asks about the hope we as Christians have within us[17]. Now, many American Christians would question whether anybody would ever ask about our hope, and given the things we'll learn in our studies, it's no wonder we'd have doubts about that. But the fact is, if we seriously practice caring love by looking for people's needs (we all have them) and finding ways to help with those needs, people who aren't Christians will soon start asking what we have that they want. And when that happens, the door's open to communicate the good news of the gospel. The Bible never encourages us to knock on doors or beat a drum on the courthouse lawn. Our job is to be ready to answer the person who asks, but we can't be ready, and they won't ask, until we learn to practice this caring love in our daily lives.

Just imagine a world where Christians really did this. Suppose that Christians traveling in foreign lands actually cared about the needs of those they met in those foreign lands. Suppose that they made preparations for a vacation abroad by finding out what they might be able to do that would be accepted gratefully wherever they were going. Think what it would be like if Christians carried the very love of God with them and shared it as Jesus did by demonstrating their willingness to give of their time and resources to help.

Can you imagine how difficult it would be to inspire terrorists to attack us if we were demonstrating that kind of love to those who were being asked to carry out the acts of terror? Can you imagine how the reaction to such love might be different from the reaction to guns and bombs? Can you imagine how people experiencing such a response to a history of terrorism might start asking what it is that motivates such love?

But beyond that, can you imagine the security this might bring if we as Christians consistently carried this kind of love to the world? And do you have any idea what the difference in cost would be? Trillions of dollars of our taxes are dedicated to protecting us from our enemies and attacking those who hurt us. But Jesus' plan is simple: "Don't let yourself be overcome by evil, but overcome evil by doing good[18]." For a tiny fraction of the cost of military might and constant vigilance, we could have far greater security than those things could ever provide and even find joy in the process.

---

[17] 1Peter 3:15.
[18] Romans 12:21.

We as Christians will never win the world to Jesus unless we learn to demonstrate in our daily lives the love that Jesus taught. It's that love that attracts people to Jesus. And when we practice that kind of love, people will ask us about the hope we have and the Lord we serve because they'll want to be part of what we have. We won't have to urge people to join with us, we'll just have to show them what it means to be part of us because that's what they'll want.

Points to Consider:
1. Seriously consider how you agree or disagree with the concept of caring love causing people to be interested in Christianity. If you experienced the kind of love described here as caring love, do you think you might want to know more about what motivated that kind of love?
2. Seriously consider some situations where Christians might legitimately want to limit their efforts to meet people's needs. Can you think of times when meeting people's physical needs might do spiritual damage?
3. Seriously consider some specific situations where Christians should be more involved in meeting needs. Are there specific areas where you believe that you should be more involved?
4. Seriously consider specific examples of how Christians might practice caring love in practical ways toward the following groups:
   a. Children struggling with schoolwork.
   b. Mothers of small children struggling with no time for themselves.
   c. People who can't figure out how to manage their money.
   d. People who might want to be Christians but can't attend church services at the times they occur.
   e. Young people who've run away from home.
   f. Have the group suggest other specific groups (there are plenty).
5. Seriously consider the idea that practicing caring love while traveling abroad could help national security. Do you think this is a real possibility?
6. Seriously consider the issue of offering help in ways that are offensive to those in need. Are there areas where you would be offended by someone offering help that you hadn't requested?

Summary Questions:
1. Did this section help you in any way, and if so, how? Be specific.

2. What do you see as the most important point or points of this section when it comes to Christians being motivated?

3. Jot down a note or two about anything you learned new in studying this section or anything you understood better because of studying this section.

CHRISTIANITY 101-A – THE GOOD NEWS OF CHRISTIAN LOVE - PART 2

CARING LOVE – OUR GOAL FOR PERSONAL GROWTH

Jesus taught his followers to think of God as their Father. In the culture of biblical times, a son was always expected to grow up and follow in the path of his father (as long as his father set a good example). Over and over the Bible makes it clear that Christianity is a growth process, and that if we're not growing as Christians, we're not Christians.

Having said this, I must admit that there are those who see good reason for questioning God's love in some of the accounts in the Bible. (If that's an important issue for members of the study group, get a copy of Revitalizing Christianity and study chapters 2, 3, and 8 after you complete this study.)

At the end of a discussion about how he was going to bring fulfillment of the Law of Moses, Jesus said, "Grow up! Show the kind of maturity that you see in your Father in heaven[1]." Jesus also said, "It's the goal of a teacher to train the mature disciples to be like their teacher[2]." During a prayer Jesus offered on his way to a garden where he would be arrested, Jesus said, "I've done all this so that they may all reach maturity, united in us, and so that the world may know for sure that you really did send me and that I care for them just as you've cared for me[3]." Sometimes growth requires drastic action. When a wealthy young man asked Jesus what he could do to assure that he would gain eternal life, Jesus replied, "If you really want to be a spiritual grown-up, here's what you need to do. Go sell all the earthly treasures you have and give to the poor. If you do that, you'll have real wealth in heaven[4]." Jesus knew that this man's wealth was blocking his growth.

Paul urged Christians to "come to the unity of the faith and of the knowledge of the son of God, to being a mature person, to measuring up to the full height of who Christ is[5]." Paul said that his goal was to "present every person mature in Christ Jesus[6]." Then Paul told these Christians how one of their own team was fervently praying "that you may stand mature and complete in all the will of God[7]."

James said, "Let patience produce its full grown result, so that you'll be mature and complete, lacking nothing[8]."

Now, if you research these verses, it'll be important to understand that in the Bible, the word often translated "perfect" also means "mature" or "full grown." There are several cases where this word's been translated as "perfect" when it's clear from the context that it can't mean true perfection, but that it can and does mean maturity.

So if we're to grow in the characteristics of our heavenly Father, we need to know what those characteristics are. The apostle John in his first letter gave us that answer: "God is caring love[9]." And if there were any doubt, Jesus' entire ministry was a demonstration of that kind of love.

The Gospels speak of Jesus' compassion both in his words and in describing what he did. When John the Immerser sent messengers to ask Jesus if he were really the Christ, Jesus' response was to say, "Those who were blind now see, those who were lame now walk, those who had leprosy are now clean, those who were deaf now hear, even those who were dead now live, and above all the poor have the good news brought to them[10]." If we're to be followers of Christ, then our lives are to be characterized by that kind of love. You may not be able to deal with physical injuries or diseases, but you certainly can carry the good news to others—however, you can only do that when you are convinced that it's really good news.

---

[1] Good News 9:69 (Matthew 5:48).
[2] Good News 35:21 (Matthew 10:29; Luke 12:6).
[3] Good News 45:20 (John 17:23).
[4] Good News 30:7 (Luke 18:22).
[5] Ephesians 4:13.
[6] Colossians 1:28.
[7] Colossians 4:12.
[8] James 1:4.
[9] 1John 4:8, 16.
[10] Good News 25:4 (Luke 7:22).

Points to Consider:

1. Seriously consider whether a person can be a Christian if he or she doesn't at least try to grow in his or her Christianity. What are your thoughts on this matter? Do you think there may be exceptions?
2. Seriously consider your personal definitions of what Christian maturity is and isn't. What aspect of Christian maturity can you think of that isn't implied in caring love as defined by Jesus?
3. Seriously consider Jesus' ministry as a demonstration of caring love. Try to go into at least some details. Do you think his condemnation of the Pharisees and Sadducees could be an expression of caring love?

CARING LOVE – THE STANDARD OF JUDGMENT

Just one time in Jesus' ministry, he described the final judgment for his disciples. At that time, Jesus went over the same information four times to emphasize his point. In the Gospels, there's only one thing Jesus emphasized more strongly in his entire ministry. This is what he told his disciples about the judgment:

"When I return in my radiant glory as a human[11] along with all the sacred agents of God, then I'll sit as king on my judgment throne[12] and all the nations will be assembled in front of me. I'll divide them as a shepherd separating his sheep from his goats. I'll have the sheep on my right side, but the goats will be sent to my left side.

"Then I'll tell those on my right side, 'Come, you who've found overwhelming joy in my Father[13], take over the kingdom we've been preparing for you since the creation of the world. It's yours because when I was hungry you gave me food, when I was thirsty you gave me something to drink, when I was a homeless stranger you took me in, when I was naked you clothed me, when I was sick you came to check up on me, and when I was in prison you visited with me[14].'

"But these righteous ones will reply, 'Lord, when did we ever see you hungry and feed you or thirsty and give you something to drink? When did we ever see you a homeless stranger and take you in or naked and clothe you? When did we ever see you sick or in prison and come to care for you[15]?'

"'I tell you the absolute truth,' I'll reply: 'as sure as you did this for just one of the very least of these who are my brothers, you did it for me.'

"Then I'll tell those on my left side, 'Get out of here[16], you who are doomed to the eternal fire prepared for Satan and his agents. This doom is yours because when I was hungry you didn't give me any food, when I was thirsty you didn't give me anything to drink, when I was a homeless stranger you didn't give me any place to stay, when I was naked you didn't provide any clothing for me, and when I was sick and in prison you never came to check on me.'

"'Lord,' they'll ask, 'When did we ever see you hungry or thirsty or a homeless stranger or naked or sick or in prison and not care for you?'

"'I tell you the absolute truth,' I'll reply: 'as sure as you failed to care for one of the very least of these who are my brothers, you failed to care for me.'

---

[11] Literally, "the son of man returns in his radiant glory…"

[12] This is the only time that Jesus told his disciples exactly what the judgment would be like—and he varied the details while repeating the same theme four times in a row for a level of emphasis exceeded only by his teaching that God's way is caring love rather than law. This is certainly one of the most important lessons Jesus taught, and the standard of judgment described is the practice of caring love.

[13] Those who find God in this world are certain to find overwhelming joy in him, no matter how much they may suffer physically.

[14] Here's what Jesus defined as the standard of God's judgment—"I was in need, and because you chose to be my servant, you cared for my need." This shouldn't be a surprise. That's caring love for others, and it's the second of the two great commandments according to Jesus. In fact, to a large degree it's how we obey the first of the two great commandments, and Jesus made that clear in this passage.

[15] For both the righteous and the wicked, the pattern of life they'd established became so natural that they didn't see it.

[16] These are words you don't want to hear from God. If you were to hear those words from God, where could you go?

"So those on the left will be condemned to eternal punishment, but those who did right will be welcomed into life everlasting[17].

William Barclay called this passage, "God's Standard of Judgment[18]," and he was right to do so. God's standard isn't like our standards. Notice that many of the things that Christian leaders claim are important aren't even mentioned in this passage. In essence, Jesus was saying that the judgment would be based on whether or not a person practiced forgiving, caring, unselfish, generous, active love toward others. This shouldn't be a surprise. Love is the first key principle of Christianity—it's the very heart and soul of Christianity. After all, it's the very essence of God, for "God is caring love[19]."

The good news here is this: when we get to heaven, the only people who'll be there will be those who've learned the lesson of caring love. We'll be surrounded by that kind of love. In this world, we can't really imagine how good that will be, but it will certainly be wonderful!

Points to Consider:
1. Seriously consider the passage quoted above as "God's Standard of Judgment." How does this compare to what you had believed previously? Does this change your previous ideas in any way? If so, what changed?
2. Seriously consider what things folks think might be issues for the judgment that are not mentioned in that passage. How important do you think those things will be for heaven? How important do you think caring love will be for heaven?
3. Seriously consider any connections you see between this standard and what heaven will be like. Do you think this fits with the idea that God is preparing us in this world for heaven?
4. Seriously consider whether heaven could be a paradise without this standard.

CARING LOVE – THE SIGN THAT WE'RE CHRISTIANS

Jesus told his disciples, "This is the very way that people will know that you're my disciples, if you truly care for each other[20]." How could he have made it any plainer? Anyone who doesn't at least try to practice this kind of Paul love toward others just isn't a Paul. Paul, by definition, have Paul's Paul in their lives. But if Paul is Paul love, then having his Paul guiding our lives must mean that Paul love guides our lives. Paul is very clear about what kind of fruit is produced if that Spirit is in a person's life:

But the fruit that the Spirit produces is caring love, joy, peace, patience, kindness, doing good, faithfulness, gentleness, self-control, etc. There's no law against those things.

And Christians have put to death their fleshly passions and all the troubles and lusts associated with those passions. If we're living in the God's Holy Spirit, let's act like it! Let's not boast about how good we are, challenging each other and envying each other[21].

---

[17] Good News 40:26-36 (Matthew 25:31-46).

[18] Page 358 of The Daily Study Bible: The Gospel of Matthew, Volume 2, Second Edition, by William Barclay, copyright 1958, published by The Westminster Press, Philadelphia.

[19] 1John 4:8 and 1John 4:16. There are those who hold that God can only be love because he's three persons and the love is between those three persons. There's no biblical support for this, and I cannot see how that can be true unless there are such differences between them that they become different gods or else God is in love with himself. Saying the words that they are three different personalities but one God doesn't make this reasonable, and nothing in the Bible indicates that this is the case. Saying that they are separate but one is just a word game—a contradiction in terms. These are words made up by men to reach political goals, and I cannot find where they are supported in the Bible. The Father is the source of all divinity. The Son is simply a very powerful extension of the Father (which is consistent with the first century concept of a son being an extension of his earthly father—so well supported biblically). The Holy Spirit's that same extension of God reaching now into our human lives. In other words, there's one God who reaches out to us in multiple ways—one God whom we experience as Father, Son, and Holy Spirit, co-eternal because they are one Spirit.

[20] Good News 42:29 (John 13:35).

[21] Galatians 5:22-26.

Notice that the first item on this list of the fruits of the Spirit is caring love. If these things are not characteristics of our daily lives, and especially the first one, then we're just not Christians. We may have our names recorded in earthly books as Christians, but our names won't be written in the Lamb's Book of Life. And again, it's OK to be a beginner just getting started, but it's not OK to be a beginner years after you started. These are the very identifying marks of a Christian.

Look once more at Paul's list of the fruits of the Holy Spirit and consider how each of these is related to the very first one. Caring love brings joy. Caring love brings peace. Caring love fosters patience and kindness. Caring love is the very definition of goodness. Caring love will, of course, be faithful. Caring love is necessarily gentle and self-controlled. You may experience something emotional and not have these things, but you can't experience the true Holy Spirit of God without having this evidence in your life.

Points to Consider:
1. Seriously consider the idea that the practice of caring love is the test of whether a person is a Christian or not. What else would you consider a necessary test for whether a person is a Christian or not?
2. Seriously consider whether it's possible to be a Christian without at least trying to grow in caring love. Do you think that might be possible given what the Bible says?
3. Seriously consider the fruits of the Spirit and whether a person can be a Christian without demonstrating growth in these characteristics. Do you think that might be possible?
4. Seriously consider the relationship between the fruits of the Spirit and caring love. Can you think of any real fruit of God's Holy Spirit that isn't directly related to caring love?

Summary Questions:
1. Did this section help you in any way, and if so, how? Be specific.

2. What do you see as the most important point or points of this section when it comes to Christians being motivated?

3. Jot down a note or two about anything you learned new in studying this section or anything you understood better because of studying this section.

CHRISTIANITY 101-B - THE OTHER SIDE OF CHRISTIAN LOVE - PART 1

"The first commandment is this:" Jesus replied, "'Listen, people of Israel! Jehovah our God— Jehovah is one! And you shall care for Jehovah your God with all your heart, with all your soul, with all your mind, and with all your strength!' That's the first and the most important commandment! The second commandment is similar to it: 'You shall care for your neighbor as you care for yourself.' There are no commandments greater than these, and these two commandments cover everything in the Law of Moses and the writings of the prophets[1]."

GOOD NEWS—BAD NEWS

In writing to the Christians in Corinth Paul said, "Now we have these three enduring factors: faith, hope, and caring love; but the greatest of these is caring love[2]." As was addressed in Christianity 101-A above, this kind of love is certainly the first key principle of Christianity. It's actually the very heart and soul of Christianity. The fact is that this can be both very good news and very bad news. Properly understood, love provides both the carrot and the stick of motivation—both motivation to want to be Christian and motivation to fear not being Christian. In this section of our study we'll look at the bad news aspect of caring love, the reason to fear not being a Christian.

Any good news is actually good only in relationship to something that's not as good, and this is true of the gospel. So to fully understand the good news, we have to understand the bad news. This doesn't make the good news any less good, it just brings out how important it is to accept that good news. In this chapter it'll be important for us to look closely at how God's message of love can be bad news when we don't live up to it.

(And by the way, the message of caring love doesn't end with this section of our study. The following sections will cover different themes, but the background of everything in this study will continue to be the caring love that's the theme of the last section and this one. The coming sections of this study will reveal more and more about caring love and God's message from many perspectives.)

Points to Consider:
1. Seriously consider the idea that any good news is only good in relation to something that's less good. Do you think this applies to Christianity? If so, in what way?

SIN AND REBELLION

In much of this section of our study we'll look at how our failure to practice caring love ("I was in need, and you didn't care enough to meet my need[3]") makes us guilty of terrible sin. As American Christians, we have a tendency to think of ourselves as the good people and the non-Christians as the bad people—people guilty of all kinds of terrible sin. As a motivational factor, this tends to cause us to be complacent. It's as if we think that we're so good that God couldn't possibly deny us access to heaven. But in this section of our study we'll find that this isn't the case at all.

Let's start with the fundamental fact that sin—any sin—is always rebellion against God, and that any rebellion against God is always sin. Even the intent to rebel against God is sin. These are just two ways of saying the same thing: sin is rebellion and rebellion is sin. Every time a person sins, that person has intentionally voted against God's rule in this world and for the rule of evil and Satan—and that's rebellion. An interesting facet of this is that if you believe that God wants you to do something and you decide not to do it, or if you believe God doesn't want you to do something and you decide to do it anyhow, even if God doesn't care one way or another about the specific item, your decision to go against what you honestly believed to be God's will is rebellion, and that's always sin.

---

[1] Good News 40:3-4 (Matthew 22:37-39; Mark 12:29-31).
[2] 1Corinthians 13:13 This translation uses the term "caring love" rather than just love because Jesus defined this word by telling the story of a Samaritan who saved the life of a dying Jew. We think of love as an emotional bond, but this kind of love doesn't necessarily involve emotion, though it can lead to an emotional bond. Instead, this caring love is a choice—a love we can and should have even toward those who are our enemies.
[3] Good News 40:26-36 (Matthew 25:31-46).

When Paul wrote his letter to the Christian team in Rome, after a brief introductory section, he immediately and dramatically shifted to the concept of sin: "The wrath of God is being revealed from heaven against all godlessness and wickedness of men who suppress the truth by their wickedness[4]." He then continued with his demonstration that "all have sinned and fall short of the glory of God[5]." When Jesus began his Sermon on the Mount, the very first thing he said was, "There's great joy for those who recognize their own spiritual poverty, because that's what it takes just to get into the kingdom of heaven[6]." This concept is borne out throughout the Bible. We cannot get into the kingdom until we realize that we're absolutely and tragically outside the kingdom—in rebellion against the King and under his condemnation. Who cries out for salvation or rescue? Isn't it those who realize that they are lost and beyond their own ability to rescue themselves? This same truth applies to Christianity as well as any other area of life. One of the serious problems of American Christianity is people who've become nominally "Christians" because that's what their family claimed to be, without ever understanding the awesome commitment involved in joining Christ's team.

This is important, and we need to look at it carefully. Paul told the Christians in Rome that before he knew God's law against coveting, he wasn't guilty of coveting, but once he knew God's law against coveting, he was trapped in sin[7]. In other words, as long as Paul didn't know God's will about coveting, he couldn't be rebelling against God, so he wasn't guilty of sin even though he coveted. It was only when he knew that he was going against God's will that his selfishness made him guilty of sin, a traitor to God's kingdom.

When Jesus was talking about spiritual blindness, some Pharisees asked if he were saying that they, too, were spiritually blind. Jesus told them that if they were truly blind, they wouldn't be guilty of sin, but since they claimed that they were not spiritually blind, they were guilty. In other words, if they couldn't see God's will, they wouldn't be guilty of sin (it wouldn't be rebellion), but since they claimed to know God's will (and certainly had access to the writings of Moses and the prophets), they were, indeed, guilty[8].

Speaking of pagans at the beginning of his letter to the Roman Christians, Paul said that they deserved God's wrath because they should have known to worship God just by looking at the creation around them, and they had not done so[9]. In other words, God wasn't going to hold them responsible for what they did if they didn't know better, but he would hold them responsible for what they certainly should have known.

And James said, "If someone knows to do good and doesn't do it, that's sin[10]." Once again the point is that it's only sin when you know (or should know) that you're going against God—you're rebelling against God. You make yourself God's enemy.

Points to Consider:
1. Seriously consider the idea that rebellion against God and sin are one and the same thing. Can you think of any sin that isn't, in some way, rebellion against God? Do you think it's fair of God to consider something sin only if the person doing that thing knows that he or she is going against God's will?
2. Seriously consider the idea that we can't hope to get into the kingdom of heaven unless we first recognize how lost we are without God's forgiveness. Can you think of a reason someone would want to be a Christian without realizing that he or she is truly condemned for rebellion against God? If so, do you think God would accept that reason?
3. Seriously consider the idea that people don't really want to be rescued until they realize a true need to be rescued. How do you think this applies to your conversion?
4. Seriously consider the idea that something is sin only when we know (or certainly should know) that we're going against God's will. Does this imply something that goes against what you've been taught before? Looking at the passages mentioned, does this seem right? Does this seem consistent with a loving God?

---

[4] Romans 1:18.
[5] Romans 3:23.
[6] Good News 9:4 (Matthew 5:3).
[7] See Romans 7:7-10.
[8] See Good News 34:36-37 (John 9:40-41).
[9] See Romans 1:18-21.
[10] James 4:17.

THE RIPTIDE OF SIN

Let's illustrate this with a story about a man we'll call Tom who lives on the west coast of Florida. Imagine that he's just retired and moved to this area, and he loves to take a specially modified inner tube and float close to the shore. He's aware that the water in this area is pretty shallow for some distance from the shore, and even if he were to have trouble, he's a good swimmer. He's aware that the tide gently pulls him away from the shore sometimes and pushes him toward the shore at other times. He's not aware that this gentle tidal flow is partly due to a long sandbar below the surface of the water about a quarter of a mile off-shore. He's not aware that an opening can develop in that sandbar or that, if an opening develops, it will cause the tide to rush out through that opening in a strong rip current.

While Tom floats, he reads a paperback novel and soaks up the sun. One day he's floating near the shore unaware that a storm during the night created an opening in the sandbar. As the tide starts to go out, he gets caught in the rip current. However, from his perspective floating in the inner tube, all he notices is that clouds in the sky seem to be moving rapidly toward shore. Tom doesn't realize that the clouds are hardly moving, while he's being drawn rapidly out to die in the sea. In this situation, although he's being pulled to certain death, he feels no danger and would never cry out for help or want to be saved.

It's only when someone on the shore cries out to get his attention that he looks up and realizes that he's in terrible danger. Tom's first thought is to paddle the inner tube toward the shore, but there's no way he can paddle fast enough while lying on the inner tube. He's a strong swimmer, so he decides to get out of the inner tube and try to swim to shore. But with his best efforts he can only hold his own against the riptide. Finally he realizes that he needs to be rescued. It's only at this point that he's ready to cry out for help—to seek salvation outside himself and his own efforts.

In the same way, until we realize that we're caught in a "riptide" of sin and that we have no hope of saving ourselves, we won't cry out for rescue and we won't be saved. Our normal first reaction to our awareness of danger will be to try to save ourselves. We may be "pretty good" people; we may be members on the role for some "church"; we may even be among the leaders for a local Christian team—if we haven't realized our hopeless state and felt the panic that will cause us to sincerely cry out for help, we cannot enter the kingdom of heaven, and there are very good reasons for this. In order to understand how desperately we need salvation, first we need to see the riptide of sin in which we're trapped.

Points to Consider:
1. Seriously consider the idea that people in need of rescue will not actively seek rescue if they don't realize the danger they're in. Do you think this would apply to people who are lost in sin in our culture today? Why, or why not?
2. Seriously consider the idea that we as American Christians tend to think of ourselves as the good people. Do you think we're justified in thinking that way? If not, why not? (Try to be specific.)

CARING LOVE AS GOD'S COMMANDMENT

Jesus said that the first and greatest of all commandments is to love God with all your heart, soul, mind, and strength; and the second commandment is to have caring love for your neighbor just as you care for yourself. He then said that everything in the Law of Moses and the writings of the prophets—that is, everything God had ever revealed of his will, hung on those two commandments[11]. In fact, in the Sermon on the Mount Jesus said that everything in the Law of Moses and the writings of the prophets could be summed up in the golden rule: "Whatever you want men to do to you, that's what you're to do to them, for this is the whole message of the Law and the prophets[12]." After all, as Jesus told his disciples close to the end of his ministry, to care for the needs of others is to care for God[13]. The best way we can show our love for God is by caring for his beloved creatures—

---

[11] See Good News 22:21-24; 40:2-7 (Matthew 22:35-40; Mark 12:28-31; Luke 10:25-28).
[12] Good News 11:15 (Matthew 7:12).
[13] Good News 40:26-36 (Matthew 25:31-46).

our fellow humans. And this isn't some hidden message in the Bible—this thought permeates the Bible, from Genesis to the Revelation.

As emphasized in the last section of this study, it's important to understand that the love Jesus talked about isn't an emotional feeling; it's a matter of choice. This love is unselfish, it cares about the needs of others, it's generous in meeting those needs and in forgiving any transgressions just as God has forgiven our transgressions, and it's active—actively responding to and providing for the needs of others. We can, and indeed Jesus commanded us to, show this kind of love to the people we emotionally hate—our enemies[14]. (In fact, one of the spiritually healthiest things a Christian can do is think about who they really don't like and then intentionally try to understand that person's needs and see what can be done to help that person—starting with prayer.)

If you consider this definition of caring love, the key is unselfishness. This doesn't mean that a Christian has no self-interest. The unselfishness of the Christian is of this world, because the Christian knows that such unselfishness in this life brings reward beyond comprehension in eternity. This love puts its faith in God to provide the reward. If you're selfish concerning this world's things, you can't really care about the needs of others or be generous or forgiving.

So since unselfishness is the core value of caring love and since failure to love is rebellion against God and therefore sin, then selfishness (including selfish pride) is the very heart and soul of sin. God has commanded us to take care of the needs of others, and we've committed treason by caring for our own wants instead of others' needs. And this world (especially since the advent of television) constantly encourages our selfishness. (One of the deepest pains of my life has been recognizing how Jesus' birthday has been turned into a holiday focused on the very selfishness that he so strongly condemned.)

Now, to avoid misunderstanding, we need to consider how this applies to pride. In our culture we're encouraged to take pride in what we do and be proud of who we are. Pride actually has two sides, one of which is good and the other is bad. It's good to take pride in being a good steward of the gifts God has given us, but it's important to remember that God's the source of all we have. We didn't choose where we'd be born, who our parents would be, or what level of wealth they would have, so we have no right to be proud of those things. We didn't choose the level of intelligence we'd have, how good or bad we'd look, how well or poorly our bodies would function, or what talents we would or wouldn't have, so we have no right to be proud of those things. We didn't choose who our childhood teachers would be or what kind of learning environment we'd have available, so we have no right to be proud of those things. It's good to take pride in being a good steward of these gifts, as long as we recall that they are gifts and that ultimately all of these gifts have their source in God. It's good to be aware of the gifts God has given us and it's fine to be aware that in some areas God has given us greater gifts than he's given most others, but it's wrong to consider ourselves inherently better than others because of these gifts or because of the abilities and opportunities we've had to develop our gifts. Pride focused on faithful stewardship of God's gifts is fine, but pride focused on seeing yourself as inherently better than others is part of the worldly selfishness that's the heart and soul of sin. It steals the honor that belongs to God, and it's therefore one more part of our rebellion.

Points to Consider:
1. Seriously consider the idea that Jesus' commandments to practice caring love toward God and toward others embody everything God ever told us. Can you think of some exception?
2. Seriously consider the idea that failure to care for the needs of others is actually rebellion against God—treason against his kingdom. Would you agree with that idea? If not, can you find any biblical support for your ideas?
3. Seriously consider the idea that selfishness about the things of this world is the heart and soul of sin. Would you agree? Try to think of sins that don't have their root in selfishness.
4. Seriously consider the two versions of pride addressed here. How would you define the difference between selfish pride and unselfish pride?

---

[14] See Good News 9:63 (Matthew 5:44; Luke 6:27, 35).

CHRISTIANITY 101-B - THE OTHER SIDE OF CHRISTIAN LOVE - PART 2

CARING LOVE AND REBELLION

"But," you may ask, "What does caring love have to do with sin?" In fact, it has everything to do with sin. If everything God ever told us to do or be can be summed up in the commandments to love God and each other, then the opposite must be true. That is, the failure to live up to this standard must be the essence of sin—rebellion against almighty God. It's not murder, stealing, adultery, and lying that constitute the essence of sin. It's not the failure to go to Christian team meetings or study our Bibles or go through the motions of Christianity. It's, instead, the failure to show unselfish, generous, active, caring love toward God and that same kind of love with forgiveness added toward anyone in need. If we practice such love, all other sins just vanish. God is caring love. If we serve caring love, we serve God. When we don't practice that kind of love, while we may avoid the things commonly thought of as sin, we can't help contributing to them, and we're still in rebellion against God.

Look again at Jesus' description of the final judgment. Those who are condemned are condemned not for what they did (such as murder, theft, abuse, lying, profanity, adultery, etc.), but for what they didn't do—for not showing caring, unselfish, generous, forgiving, active love—for not meeting the needs of those in need. And if you think about it, if those who are condemned had been showing this kind of love, the other sins could never have happened. How can you murder someone or steal from someone or commit adultery with someone if you're seeking what's best for others? All these things that are considered worse sins are the result of selfishness.

To illustrate the point, let's say that a division of the army has been ordered to take a particular section of ground from the enemy. If the commander reports back that his troops have killed a thousand enemy soldiers in areas unrelated to his orders, but that the area he was ordered to take hasn't been touched yet, that commander should be removed from command. Similarly, if we fight against all the popular definitions of sin (rape, murder, abuse, theft, etc.) and don't practice caring, unselfish, generous, forgiving, active love, we're still in rebellion, traitors to God's kingdom.

We need to give this some careful thought. If I get up in the morning and I treat other family members improperly (unnecessary anger, harsh words, sullen behavior, etc.), or if I just fail to be as caring and forgiving as I should, I've sinned and I'm in rebellion against almighty God. I've voted for Satan to rule this world instead of God, because that's how Satan wants me to act. If I treat fellow employees at work in a way that doesn't communicate caring, unselfish, generous, forgiving, active love, I've sinned. And my sin is just as bad as murder, because it can actually result in murder. Not that I'd physically murder anyone, but that I may cause an expanding influence of ill will that results in someone else committing murder. While that other person is directly guilty, in God's eyes, I'd be an accessory just as guilty as the murderer, for if I had demonstrated caring love toward the person with whom I was dealing, the murderer might never have reached the point where he or she felt compelled to murder. I may have been just one small influence on the murderer, but if I contributed to the circumstances that brought about the murder, I'm still guilty as an accomplice. From God's perspective, this is reality. (Even our human legal systems have a similar standard concerning accessories to a crime, though our legal standards can't be implemented to the extent that God's standard is.)

Husbands, do you ever knowingly and intentionally say or do things that will hurt your wives? Wives, do you ever knowingly and intentionally say or do things that will hurt your husbands? If you do, that's rebellion against God Almighty. You probably even swore before God and witnesses that you would love, honor, and cherish your spouse as long as both of you live. How can we think that it's OK to cast aside those vows and turn them all into lies by treating our marriage partners badly—no matter how much they may deserve such treatment? Our vows said nothing about contingencies.

Parents hurt their children, children hurt their parents, brothers and sisters hurt each other, Christians hurt each other—and we do it knowingly and intentionally. All of this is rebellion against Almighty God. We who are supposed to be his beloved children become traitors—enemies of his kingdom. We refuse to submit to him and do as he has told us to do, even though we know that his standard is good and right.

And then there's road rage. Someone cuts you off in traffic, someone blows his or her horn at you in traffic, or someone just doesn't drive the way you think that person should drive in that situation—and suddenly you allow Satan to direct your thoughts and actions. All of this is rebellion against Almighty God. We're caught in this riptide of sin! And the riptide's pulling us into the eternal torment of hell.

Am I trying to scare people into heaven? Absolutely! Read the Bible and you'll find the same approach. "The fear of Jehovah God is the very beginning of understanding, but fools despise wisdom and instruction[1]." If there were no threat of hell, few if any would ever find the blessings of Christianity and heaven. However, scaring people into conversion doesn't work unless there's an immediate follow-up with a discipleship program that provides the positive motivations of Christianity. As the apostle John said in his first letter, "There's no fear in caring love, but mature caring love drives away all fear[2]." Once we start living with our hearts focused on caring love for others, the joy will just keep growing while the fear will be absolutely banished. The threat of hell is the stick that motivates most people to come into the kingdom, but the joys of the kingdom are the carrot that keeps them growing and keeps the kingdom growing.

When we see ourselves in this perspective as rebels against God and his kingdom, when we realize that we're traitors to the kingdom every time we react in an unforgiving or an uncaring way toward those around us who are in need, then we begin to understand the terrible state of our rebellion. And God's response isn't gentle understanding and generous forgiveness—it's adamant rejection of our selfish worldliness. In our natural state of rebellion, God cannot and will not allow us into his eternity, because if he were to do so, we'd bring the ruin of rebellion with us. And there's no middle ground. As Jesus put it, "He who isn't with me is against me, and he who doesn't gather the harvest with me scatters it[3]."

Picture a football team on the field for an important game. The coach has sent orders that are clear, and each player knows his job. Now suppose that one of the players decides that he just doesn't feel like participating, so he stays out of the way of the opposing team to make sure he doesn't get hurt. This player likes to dress in the uniform. He loves the attention he gets from the other students and especially from the cheerleaders. He just doesn't want to risk any injury that might make him less attractive to his fans. The actions of that player would likely allow the opposing team to win the game. No coach would tolerate such a player on his team.

The same is true for Christians. In any Christian team there are always some who enjoy looking like they're part of God's team, but they don't participate in the game (which for Christians is much more than a game). Our failure to show unselfish, caring, generous, forgiving, active love when we could easily have done so can result in others never accepting the gospel. Don't forget, caring love is God's tool for evangelism. So our failure to do as we've been commanded to do by our Lord is sure to result in someone God loves going into eternal torment. That's a whole lot worse than murder, and we're guilty when we don't practice the caring love God's commanded us to practice! In addition, such failures can result in the enemy being able to accuse God's people of not showing love, which results in more people being lost. When some of God's people don't show the love of God, they dishonor God and discredit his people as a whole—and Satan rejoices whenever Christianity gets a bad reputation.

Remember, sin is rebellion against God Almighty, and if unforgiven, it's punishable by hell (which is far worse than anything you or I can imagine). God has told us how he wants us to live, and when we decide to live in a different manner, we're in rebellion against God. We become traitors to his cause. God's anger, his wrath, is being revealed from heaven against those who are in rebellion[4]. After all, it's those in rebellion who've caused the death of Jesus—just as surely as if they'd pounded the nails in and thrown the spear. And it's those in rebellion who are sending millions to hell without a clue about the gospel message.

As Hebrews says, "It's a fearful thing to fall into the hands of the living God[5]." This isn't a game. It's the most serious accusation we could face. We've been warned that we'll have to stand trial before the highest court in all eternity on the charge of murder—of causing the crucifixion of the Ultimate Judge's son. There's no escape, there's no bail, and there's no defense we can offer. Our only hope is the grace of God, and that only applies if we've decided to end our rebellion and truly join God's side.

---

[1] Proverbs 1:7.
[2] 1John 4:18.
[3] Good News 17:67 (Matthew 12:30 or Luke 11:23).
[4] Romans 1:18.
[5] Hebrews 10:31.

Points to Consider:
1. Seriously consider the idea of our failure to practice caring love as being rebellion against God—as joining Satan's side. Does that make sense to you? If not, what seems wrong with the picture presented? Is there a something in the Bible that shows this to be wrong?
2. Seriously consider the idea that the failure to practice caring love is a root cause of sins we often think of as far more serious. Can you name any sin that isn't caused by some failure to practice caring love?
3. Seriously consider the idea that the failure of Christians to practice caring love makes them accessories to things like murder, theft, and such. Try to think from God's perspective. Does this make sense?
4. Seriously consider the distinction between a Christian who is focused on practicing caring love and one who is more focused on externals and being seen by the world as a Christian. Which one do you think God will accept?
5. Seriously consider how you might feel if you found out that someone's intentional neglect of reasonable responsibilities had led to the death of your child. How do you think that might apply to God?

NO HOPE OF PAYMENT

When we see that our failure to help others where God would reasonably expect us to help is treason against God's kingdom, we should realize that each of us is guilty and in terrible trouble. Furthermore, we need to realize that there's nothing we can do to compensate for even one sin. Once you've committed treason, you're a traitor. Even our own legal systems have this perspective. Many people believe that if they do enough good deeds, the good deeds will balance the bad ones and they'll get into heaven. This is just not true—it's not even true in the legal systems of a worldly country.

Jesus told his disciples of a slave owner who sent his slave to work in the field all day and then had him prepare the evening meal and serve him. The slave had no permission to eat or rest until his field work had been done and the master had been fed. And the master didn't thank him, because the slave had just done what he was supposed to do[6]. In the same way, Jesus told his disciples that even when they'd done everything they should have done, they should still consider themselves as slaves who brought their master no profit, because they'd only done what they were required to do.

The lesson of this story is that even if we could do everything God ever wanted us to do, we wouldn't have earned any credit—we'd only have done what we were created to do. That might be adequate to get us into heaven if we could do that, but none of us can. And there's nothing we can possibly do for "extra credit." If we spent every moment of our lives doing everything we could possibly do for God, we'd simply be "breaking even." The first failure is disastrous rebellion. With that first failure, we join Satan's side and he claims us as his own.

From God's perspective, the difference between a murderer and someone who fails to show caring, unselfish, generous, forgiving, active love toward others is practically insignificant. Both are in rebellion. Both have chosen Satan's side. Both are under condemnation. Both are guilty of causing the death of Jesus on the cross. This is the great leveler of Christianity, and it's important for every Christian to see and understand this truth. Too many of those who attend church want to be like Jack Horner, to stick in a finger and say, "What a good person I am."

This is also the point of Jesus' story about two debtors—one who owed more than any man could repay, and the other who owed a relatively small amount. In this story, Jesus told of a king who wished to settle accounts with his slaves. (In New Testament times, every subject of a kingdom was considered a slave of the king.) One of his slaves owed (in terms of the early 21st century) about 5 billion dollars. Since the slave couldn't repay this debt, the king ordered that everything the man had should be confiscated and the man and his family should be sold as slaves. But when the man begged for time to repay, the king said he would actually forgive the entire debt. In Jesus' story, the king's slave then found a fellow slave who owed him the equivalent of about $10,000. Since this man couldn't pay his debt, the slave whose debt had been so generously forgiven had this debtor thrown into prison. But when the king heard of this, he reinstated the first slave's debt and sent him to the torture chambers until he could pay off the whole debt[7].

---

[6] Good News 21:1-4 (Luke 17:7-10).
[7] Good News 22:1-15 (Matthew 18:23-35).

No one can pay for a sin against God or against anyone else. You cannot un-sin a sin. By caring for someone in need, you cannot make up for not caring for someone else you chose to neglect. In Jesus' story, both men were debtors who couldn't repay their debts—the only difference was how big the debt was. Once we understand how big our debt is and how impossible repayment is, there can be no excuse for not forgiving the much smaller debts of those who sin against us. When we see our debt as greater than anything we could ever hope to repay, only then can we realize just how much we need the awesome grace and mercy of God.

Look at this from God's perspective. How many thieves would have become thieves if Christians had paid attention to their needs and seen to it that those needs were properly met? How many murderers would have become murderers if Christians had done the work God commanded them to do? How many who've committed adultery would never have done so if their spouses had practiced caring love toward them[9]? God knows these answers. He knows that our neglect of others has made us accessories to the things we consider "bad" sins.

Each one of us is caught in a riptide of sin, and we all need God's grace to rescue us, but not one of us could ever pay for that rescue. When we realize how much God has forgiven us, we must be driven to be gracious and merciful and caring toward others. If that doesn't happen, we're simply adding new sins to our old sins, and God won't forgive either one because forgiving such a person would produce no benefit.

The common response of a person who refuses to forgive is something like, "But you don't know what they did to me!" Once we understand what our rebellion has done to God, how it has contributed to God's beloved creatures being condemned to hell and to the death of God's beloved son, how can we refuse forgiveness to others? How easily God could say of us, "But you don't know what they did to me!" and point to the cross.

Points to Consider:
1. Seriously consider the idea that a slave can never do anything that would be considered more than he or she should do as a slave. How can this apply to us as God's creations? Do you think this is a fair assessment?
2. Seriously consider the idea that, from God's perspective, both a murderer and someone who doesn't practice caring love are rebels and therefore subject to condemnation. In light of the cross, does this seem reasonable?
3. Seriously consider the idea that if God allowed rebels into heaven they would bring their rebellion with them and ruin heaven. Does that seem realistic?
4. Seriously consider the comparison between what we have done to God by neglecting to care for others whom he created and whom he loves versus what others have done to hurt us. How does this apply to our willingness to forgive those who hurt us?

DOES PRACTICING LOVE PAY FOR SINS?

As a part of this topic, we need to address something Peter wrote: "And above all else have earnest caring love for one another, because caring love covers many, many sins[8]." This passage is often thought of as teaching that we can pay for a lot of our sins just by loving others, and the words Peter used could be understood that way. However, these same words can mean that practicing love will inherently keep us from a large number of sins. Putting this concept another way, teaching people to practice caring love will inherently cause them to avoid a whole lot of sins—the topic of caring love actually covers every topic of sin. Letting the Bible interpret the Bible, the latter meaning is consistent with what Jesus taught, and is also consistent with the context in Peter's letter. We cannot pay for any of our sins—not even one, and to avoid sin, we need to practice caring love.

Points to Consider:
1. Seriously consider the idea that teaching and practicing caring love can deal with ("cover") many sins. Does this make sense to you?

THE PERSPECTIVE OF SATAN

One of the most serious dangers for Christians is to think of sin the way Satan wants us to think of sin. He would have us focus on the sins of others as "real" sin, while our own sins are classified as minor or insignificant. He would have us focus on murder, abortion, adultery, homosexuality, pornography, drunkenness, dope addiction,

---

[8] 1Peter 4:8.

drug pushing, robbery, idolatry, abusiveness, gambling, profanity, etc. He wouldn't have us focus on gossip, arrogance, boastfulness, faithlessness, ruthlessness, deceitfulness, malice, envy, pride, greed, and the other sins we do commit, lest we see our danger and repent. Yet, when Paul listed the sins that bring God's wrath[9], he included all of these—the ones we think of as bad, and the ones we don't want to think about. Even apathy to the needs of others is rebellion against God.

And remember, it only takes one sin to make any of us a traitor and bring about our condemnation before God. Just one sin puts us in Satan's camp and in rebellion against God. Once we rebel against God, we're on Satan's side and we stand under the same condemnation that he faces.

We need to see the lies in Satan's arguments. We need to understand that we're truly and seriously condemned to hell on our own, and that our only chance of salvation is God's grace. And we need to understand that God's grace is dependent on our faith, which means ending our rebellion.

Points to Consider:
1. Go through the list of sins that Satan doesn't want us to think of as "bad sins." Seriously consider how these sins might contribute to other sins that we do think of as the "bad sins." How might this affect God's view of the sins we do commit?
2. Think through the topic of caring love that we've just covered. In what ways, if any, has this changed your perspective on Christianity?

Summary Questions:
1. Did this section help you in any way, and if so, how? Be specific.

2. What do you see as the most important point or points of this section when it comes to Christians being motivated?

3. Jot down a note or two about anything you learned new in studying this section or anything you understood better because of studying this section.

---

[9] See Romans 1:29-31.

CHRISTIANITY 102 – FAITH—THE ULTIMATE FOCUS - PART 1

Without faith it's impossible to please God,
because anyone who comes to him must believe that he exists
and that he rewards those who sincerely seek him[1].

Let's focus once again on Paul's words to the Christians in Corinth: "Now we have these three enduring factors: faith, hope, and caring love; but the greatest of these is caring love[2]." Love is certainly the first key principle of Christianity, but faith is a very close second. As Paul wrote to the Christians in Rome, "So it's obvious that a man is justified by faith, completely separate from keeping the Law given by Moses[3]." Faith is the key to the door into heaven, but to have the key, we must learn what Christian faith or belief really is. And surprisingly, most Christian groups get that definition wrong even though the Bible is very clear.

Most of us as Christians know that there's some link between Christian faith and Christian belief, but we're not entirely clear about that link. Many think that faith is a stronger form of belief or that it adds something to belief. Understanding the reality of that link is very important, and for most it's also very surprising.

On the surface, belief seems a simple enough concept, but there's a problem that's plagued Christians from the very beginning. The problem is that the word "belief" has a very wide range of meanings in English and an even wider range of meanings in the language of the New Testament. Satan wants us to get the wrong meaning. Once we learn what the Bible authors meant when they used their word for belief, we'll find that this too can be highly motivating. (God truly knows how to motivate, but Satan specializes in distracting us from the motivation God provides.)

Points to Consider:
1. Seriously consider briefly what you think of as the difference between "faith" and "belief" as these apply to Christianity. Write out your idea of the difference in meaning between these two words as used in the Bible.

JUST ONE WORD FOR 'FAITH' AND 'BELIEF'

Now it's important to understand that the Bible word translated 'belief' is always the same as the word translated 'faith.' There's absolutely no distinction between these terms in the Bible[4]. This word appears as a verb (to believe or to have faith) and as a noun (belief or faith), but it's clearly the same word every time. The person who translates the Bible into English chooses whether he or she will translate this word as "faith" or as "belief." (Strangely, the translators of the King James Version of the Bible used the word 'faith' wherever the noun form appeared and the word 'believe' wherever the verb form appeared, intentionally or unintentionally implying some difference in meaning, but this doesn't serve well to communicate the intent of those who wrote the New Testament.)

In English, belief can mean as little as a casual belief on which you'd take no action, such as a belief that the coming winter will be a wet one. It can also mean a firm conviction on which you'd take action, but with a lack of certainty, such as belief that a certain stock you're about to purchase will increase in value. It can mean a conviction on which you'll take action and which you're quite certain will prove true, as when you get on an airplane to visit a city you've never visited before. You believe that the city is there and that the airplane will take you to that city, even though you've never seen the city and know nothing about how an airplane works.

However, a less common English meaning for "belief" is important for understanding the New Testament concept. In English a person may say, "You've got to have something to believe in," meaning, "You need to have some core principle on which you base every decision in your life."

---

[1] Hebrews 11:6.
[2] 1Corinthians 13:13
[3] Romans 3:28
[4] For those who are interested, the Greek term used in the New Testament is "*pistis*" in the noun form (belief or faith) and "*pisteuein*" in the verb form (to believe or to have faith).

When we use that phrase, we're talking about something we believe so strongly that we'd never willingly do anything that would violate that belief. Such a belief shapes how we think, what we say, and what we do. If a person has that kind of belief in Jesus, such a belief would be equivalent to saying "Jesus is Lord—and specifically Lord of my life. Everything I say, do, and think will be shaped by who he is and what he would want."

If you're at all familiar with Christianity, you may already be ahead of the story here as you realize that this meaning is important in understanding how Christian faith (or belief) and Christian works go together. We'll find that this kind of belief is what Jesus taught, what Paul taught, what James taught, and, indeed, what every New Testament author taught. This so permeates the New Testament, and really the whole Bible, that once we grasp this it's hard to see how anyone could ever have missed it. In the New Testament, this kind of core belief is what's meant whenever faith or belief is mentioned relative to salvation with only one exception. That exception was specifically intended to reinforce this meaning. (We'll come to that in a little bit.)

In fact, from the beginning of Genesis to the end of the Revelation, the most consistent message of the Bible is that we as humans must accept God's divine authority over our lives if we hope to survive the judgment. Lip service won't do. Jesus said that many would call him "Lord, Lord," but he would have nothing to do with them[5]. Appearance without substance won't do. In that same passage, Jesus said that many would claim to have served him in various ways including prophecy and miracles, but he would have nothing to do with them. Saving faith or belief is a refocusing of our lives, a shift in focus from ourselves and the things of this world to God and the things of his kingdom. It's the end of our rebellion. Nothing else will do, and we'll learn why before we complete this study.

When we understand that saving belief involves reshaping one's life around one's belief, we can understand the whole Bible message better. To believe in the gospel is to shape one's life around the message of the gospel. It involves believing God's message, and making every thought and action conform to that belief. This has a lot to do with motivation, because it involves finding our motivation in serving God.

As we learned in the last two sections of this study, God has provided a message that's motivating. (We'll learn much more about how motivating that message is throughout this study.) The motivations we focused on in earlier sections of this study were the joy of living with caring love the fear of hell for those who don't practice caring love, but there's much more. For now we need to understand that faith involves intentionally setting our sights on the goal of serving God and then using that goal to shape our lives. For the Christian, God's will as demonstrated and taught by Jesus and his followers becomes the ultimate goal.

As mentioned above, the New Testament word for faith or belief has an even wider range of meaning than the English. For Jesus and his followers, this one word could mean "trust," "conviction," "assurance," and various others not generally associated with the English words. As we'll see shortly, a careful study of the biblical use of this term will lead you to the conclusion that the most common meaning for Jesus and his followers was the meaning we have in English when we say, "You've got to have something to believe in"—that core belief that shapes every action, word, and thought in your life. Such a belief in God is effectively an end to the rebellion of sin. We'll still sin, but the sin will be in spite of our consistent effort to live for God. Our aim shifts from the worldly to the eternal, from the physical to the spiritual.

Points to Consider:
1. Seriously consider how your thoughts about "faith" and "belief" might be changed based on the fact that, in the Bible, these two are actually the same word. How do you think this should change the way we think of salvation?
2. Seriously consider the concept of the English saying, "You've got to have something to believe in," and how this might apply to Christian faith or belief. What would those words mean for you?
3. Seriously consider the concept that faith or belief is a focusing of your life on serving God and is the theme of the whole Bible. Do you agree with that concept? Explain your perspective.
4. Seriously consider the idea that this understanding of faith or belief can harmonize the emphasis Jesus placed on "belief" or "faith" and the emphasis he placed on how people live. Does that make sense to you?

---

[5] Good News 11:37-40 (Matthew 7:21-23; Luke 6:46)

5. Seriously consider the difference between the motivation of hell (the desire to avoid hell) and the motivation of faith (the desire to focus your life on God). Which one do you think would provide the initial motivation most likely to have the results God would want? Which one would be more likely to motivate for the long term?

WHAT JESUS SAID ABOUT FAITH/BELIEF

In John's Gospel, Jesus is quoted as saying,

> I'm telling you the absolute truth: those who seriously listen to what I teach and put their faith in the Father who sent me already have life everlasting. These won't have to face judgment. They've already passed from death into eternal life. Again I'm telling you the absolute truth: the time's coming - in fact it's already here - when the dead will hear my voice, the voice of God's own son, and those who listen to me will live forever[6]. Just as life itself is an inherent part of who my Father is, so he's granted me as his son to have life inherently in myself. He's given me authority to mete out justice because I've lived here as a human and experienced what it is to be human[7]. Does this surprise you? I tell you, the time's coming when everyone in the graves will hear my voice and come out. Those who've done what's good will rise to life everlasting. Those who've done what's wrong will rise to find themselves condemned eternally. Now, by myself I can't do anything[8]. I judge people based on what I hear, and my judgment is right because I'm not looking out for my own interests, but for what my Father (the one who sent me) wants[9].

Notice the following two phrases in this paragraph: 1) "Those who seriously listen to what I teach and put their faith in [believe in] the Father who sent me already have life everlasting"; and 2) " Those who've done what's good will rise to life everlasting. Those who've done what's wrong will rise to find themselves condemned eternally." In this passage, Jesus says two things that may, at first, seem to be contradictory. First, he says that eternal life depends on believing or having faith in "the one who sent me." Second, he says that the dead will be raised to judgment, and the judgment will be based on what they've done. So is the judgment based on belief (faith) or on works?

These concepts would be conflicting if "believe" meant just believing facts or trusting Christ to save. If a person has eternal life just by believing God, how can that person be judged eternally based on what he or she's done? However, if "believe" means focusing one's life on the one believed in, then the passage makes sense because such a belief would cause a person to do the good things that God wants him or her to do. In God's perspective, you cannot truly believe in him if you don't live as if you truly believe. To claim that we believe one thing while living as if we believe something else is simply to lie.

But more significantly, in the message we know as the Sermon on the Mount, early in the sermon Jesus contrasted the way of laws and rules with God's way. In that passage, Jesus went over six different areas of life where Jewish religious leaders taught laws or rules that Jews generally considered God's rules for how to live, and in each case Jesus made it clear that the message he brought was not about living up to the rules, but rather it was about focusing your life on God so completely that the rules became unnecessary[10]. There's nothing else in Jesus' ministry that he emphasized as powerfully as that message.

---

[6] Jesus repeatedly made the point that as Christians, we don't die. Our bodies are left behind, but the reality of our selves—the soul—takes on a new body that lasts forever.

[7] Literally, "because he's the son of man."

[8] Here Jesus separates his human self—the self that can do nothing, from the spiritual presence of God within him with unlimited power.

[9] Good News 28:24-29 (John 5:25-30).

[10] Good News 9:34-68 (Matthew 5:21-47).

Points to Consider:
1. Seriously consider Jesus words about being judged by our faith versus being judged according to our works. Does the concept of belief or faith presented in this study work to show how these two statements can both be true? Can you come up with another way to harmonize these two statements?
2. Review Good News 9:33-69 (Matthew 5:20-48) and seriously consider how this passage fits with the definition of biblical faith or belief presented in this study.

WHAT PAUL SAID ABOUT FAITH/BELIEF

Paul wrote to the Christians in Rome saying, "Therefore it's obvious that a man is justified by faith [belief], completely separate from keeping the Law given by Moses[11]." This might seem to argue that believing certain things is the basis of salvation. However, three verses later Paul wrote, "Do we, then, nullify the Law of Moses by this faith? May that thought never even form in your mind! On the contrary, we uphold the law[12]." Yet, if belief (or faith) in the facts of who Jesus really is truly saves us, then we'd make the law of no real significance. If a "sinner's prayer" really and permanently saves us, then we're saved whether or not we live in accordance with rules or laws. However, if the belief or faith Paul wrote about was a founding principle on which we make all of our life decisions, if that faith means focusing our lives on God's will, then these concepts are compatible.

Our faith or belief causes us to live up to the moral principles of God's Law even though living by God's Law could never earn us anything once we break that law one time. We live up to the intent of the law not to earn anything, but to live out our devotion to God. By this kind of faith we'll simply have ended our rebellion, and then God's grace will wipe out our guilt. As Christians, we don't follow the guidance of the law because it's law and there's some penalty for disobedience, but because we love God and have entrusted our entire lives to him—his will has become the internal motivation for our lives. Believing that Jesus came as God's son and died for our sins doesn't "uphold the law," but reshaping our lives around the message Jesus brought does cause us to live up to the moral intent of the law.

Points to Consider:
1. Seriously consider Paul's words about faith upholding the law. Can you find a way that this would be true other than the one suggested in this study?

WHAT JAMES SAID ABOUT FAITH/BELIEF

James has often been perceived as in disagreement with Paul. After all, Paul taught that "a man is justified by faith [belief], completely separate from keeping the law[13]," while James taught that, "In the same way, faith [belief] by itself, if it isn't accompanied by appropriate action, is dead[14]." Yet, each of these New Testament authors defined how they were using the word "faith." As we saw, what Paul wrote to the Roman Christians effectively defined "faith" as necessarily involving living up to the intent of the law (therefore a core motivational belief that shapes one's life). But James wrote, "My brothers, what good is it if a man claims to have faith [belief] but has no deeds? Can faith [belief] like that save him[15]?" In the New Testament, James is the only one who doesn't use the word "faith" to mean a focusing of your life on God. By what he wrote implying that the "faith" he's talking about doesn't result in action, James shows that he's using "faith" to mean "acceptance of facts as true" without a change in the focus of one's life, and that was a valid meaning for this biblical word. James uses this definition of faith (and makes it very clear that this is the definition he's using) in order to show that this kind of "faith" is not saving faith.

Thus, using the definition Paul and Jesus used, faith saves us all by itself because it results in a changed life, but using the definition James used, faith as belief in facts by itself doesn't affect how we live and cannot save us.

---

[11] Romans 3:28.
[12] Romans 3:31.
[13] Romans 3:28.
[14] James 2:20.
[15] James 2:14.

Don't let the definitions become too confusing. The point is that faith isn't saving faith and belief isn't saving belief unless that faith or belief is a motivational factor that shapes how you live.

Points to Consider:
1. Seriously consider James' words about faith by itself not bringing salvation. Can you find a way that this would be true and still match what Jesus and Paul said other than the one suggested in this study? Does the idea suggested in this study seem valid in light of what James wrote?

WHAT THE BIBLE SAYS IN HEBREWS ABOUT FAITH/BELIEF

As a last example, in Hebrews we read,

> Now with whom was he [God] angry for forty years? Wasn't it with those who sinned, whose bodies fell in the wilderness? And to whom did he [God] swear that they wouldn't enter his rest? Wasn't it to those who disobeyed? So we see that they couldn't enter his rest because of unbelief[16].

In this passage, notice how "those who disobeyed" are the same as those who "couldn't enter his rest because of unbelief." Disobedience and unbelief are treated as exactly equivalent. And that same usage of these terms as exactly equivalent continues in chapter 4. Once again we see that early Christians defined belief as something that would necessarily shape how we live. The one who wrote this passage couldn't think of faith (belief) as separate from obedience. For him, those who have faith would be faithful, and those who were not faithful must not have faith.

Points to Consider:
1. Seriously consider this passage from Hebrews. Does the author's use of unbelief and disobedience seem to imply what this study suggests? Can you think of another way to understand this passage?
2. Combining what these passages from Jesus, Paul, James, and Hebrews say, how would you define saving faith?

Summary Questions:
1. Did this section help you in any way, and if so, how? Be specific.

2. What do you see as the most important point or points of this section when it comes to Christians being motivated?

3. Jot down a note or two about anything you learned new in studying this section or anything you understood better because of studying this section.

---

[16] Hebrews 3:18-19.

CHRISTIANITY 102 – FAITH—THE ULTIMATE FOCUS - PART 2

LAW AND FAITH IN CHRISTIANITY

At times the news media have pushed some of our buttons as Christians when it comes to the Bible and God's Law. At least for a time, the Ten Commandments became a hot button issue, and in many parts of the country you could see signs with the Ten Commandments in Christians' yards as if this were an essential part of Christianity. Indeed, there are ways in which this is at least partially true, but one of the strongest themes in the New Testament is that Christians aren't under law—any law—as far as God's concerned. Accepting Jesus as Lord doesn't mean a new set of laws and more guilt for failing to live up to those laws. This doesn't mean that Christians can simply ignore God's will for their lives—quite the contrary. But it does mean that there's no law, not the Ten Commandments, not the Law given by God through Moses, and not any New Testament list of do and don't items. It's more like "Do your best for God and trust God to deal with the rest." The "do your best for God" part consists of ending the rebellion and focusing your life on living for God—that core belief we've been describing. As a Christian named Augustine once put it, "Love God, and then do whatever you want." Because if we truly love God, we'll want to do what he wants us to do.

As God knew from the beginning, one problem with law is that people can always find a way around almost any law. For example, if God's law says "You shall not bear false witness," we find a way to say only things that are true while intentionally implying something entirely false. (Who hasn't done this and then claimed, "I didn't *lie*"?)

Another problem with law is that people justify their law-breaking with the rationale that others who are supposed to be good people do worse than they are doing. (This is like claiming that you shouldn't be gaining weight when you eat too much as long as someone near you is eating more.) Or people excuse themselves because they are doing some sort of penance to make up for violating a law or rule; or people are sacrificing in some way that makes it OK for them to break the laws and rules.

In over a thousand years of having God's law, by the time of Jesus' ministry, the Jews still hadn't come to truly honor God's law with their lives in the way God intended. In nearly two thousand years since that time, this is still true. People may strictly observe traditions that were intended to meet the requirements of the law, but the more strictly they observe the traditions, the more blatantly they miss the real intent of the law.

Yet another problem with law is that it encourages people to do the least necessary to keep the law. But God has no pleasure in those who seek the least—he accepts those who seek to do all they can with no regard to what the minimum is. Today, those who ask "What must I do to be saved?" often mean "What is the least I can get by with in order to avoid hell." Anyone looking for the minimum is looking in the wrong direction, and such a person is almost certainly lost. God is looking for a faith that says, "How much more can I do?" After all, if we love God, that will be our attitude—and for Christians, loving God is the first commandment.

Who doesn't break the laws of our country? Most of us who drive break the speed limits or roll through stop signs. Reports in the news indicate that large numbers of those who can find a way to do so somehow cheat on their taxes. Those who purchase products by mail or Internet without paying sales tax are almost always in violation of state laws. Whatever the laws say, we find ways to cheat on the laws. God doesn't want law-abiding followers; he wants followers who've given their hearts and lives to serving him in such a way that laws and rules become superfluous.

I've heard professional Christian leaders and Bible professors say that God's law can be divided into two or three groups for Christian application. If the division is into two groups, it's generally something like "dispensational laws" and "eternal laws" with the implication that the dispensational laws went away when Jesus died but the eternal laws still apply to Christians. The Bible never divides God's laws into dispensational and eternal, so how can we possibly know which laws are supposed to be dispensational and which are supposed to be eternal? If we don't know, how can we ever be certain of our salvation?

For those who identify three groups of laws the divisions are generally along the lines of "ceremonial laws," "civil laws," and "moral laws," with only the moral laws being viewed as applicable to Christians. The Bible never uses these terms or teaches anything like that. Again, how can we know which laws apply to us and which do not? One pastor or professor will teach one list, and another teaches a different list. How can we find peace if

31

we can't determine what laws apply to Christians? We can thank God that these questions aren't a problem for Christians, because salvation is by faith, not by laws and rules.

At the beginning of his account of Jesus' ministry, Matthew recorded a lengthy and awesome sermon we call the Sermon on the Mount. This message contains many of Jesus' most important teachings, and there can be no doubt that the topics covered in this sermon were common threads in Jesus' teachings throughout his ministry. Early in this sermon, Jesus told his followers

> Don't even think that I've come to tear down the Law of Moses and the things taught by the prophets. My purpose isn't to tear down what those men wrote, but to give full meaning to their messages. I assure you that this is the absolute truth: even the smallest stroke of a pen in the Law of Moses still applies until everything in that Law is given its full meaning[1]. Therefore, if someone violates even one of the least significant commandments in the Law of Moses and influences others to do the same, that person shall be considered the lowest in rank in the kingdom of heaven. But if someone lives by those teachings and influences others to do the same, that person will be considered great in the kingdom of heaven[2]. I'm telling you: unless your goodness is better than the 'goodness' of the scribes and the Pharisees, you won't even get into the kingdom of heaven[3].

Jesus followed this statement with a list of legalistic things that were taught by the religious leaders (scribes, Pharisees, etc.) of his time, and in each case he demonstrated that the fulfillment he was talking about was a matter of the spirit of the law rather than the letter of the law. In fact, in some cases Jesus actually reversed what a specific written law said to focus on the overriding spirit or principles behind the whole Law of Moses. In other words, the fulfillment of the law that Jesus said he came to bring actually did away with the law as law and replaced it with a life of faith demonstrated by dedication to God and his intent. As we saw earlier, the fact that the judgment will be about people having learned to practice caring love is the teaching Jesus emphasized more strongly than any other except one—and this is the one. In this passage we learn how Jesus went over this same basic principle six times in a row, and the point was consistently the same: Christianity is not about laws and rules, it's about a life of faith that is so dedicated to living according to the principles of caring love that no laws or rules are needed.

For Christians there are three important keys in what Jesus said in this chapter: 1) either the entire law (down to the least mark on the page) applies to Christians, including laws of sacrifice, Sabbath laws, civil laws, and moral laws; or else all of God's Law from the Ten Commandments down to the most detailed ceremonial law has been fulfilled by Jesus' teachings about faith as focusing on doing God's will (which is exactly what Jesus said he had come to do); 2) for Christians, God's Law has been superseded by a commandment to love God with an unselfish, caring, generous, active love, meaning that we'll do what the spirit of the Law teaches, not because it's law, but because we've given our hearts to pleasing God; and 3) we aren't expected to be fully perfect, but we're required to grow toward the spiritual maturity we find in God.

Jesus' conclusion was, "Grow up! Show the kind of maturity that you see in your Father in heaven[4]." As noted in the footnote, this verse is often misunderstood, but the meaning Jesus was communicating was all about discipleship—growing spiritually into the image of our Heavenly Father.

---

[1] Note that Jesus said that nothing in the Law of Moses would go away until everything in it was given its full meaning, but that he'd come to do exactly that. In other words, if we accept the fulfillment of the law that Jesus brought—a life focused on living for God—that law doesn't apply, but if not, everything in that law still applies.

[2] Given what Jesus said later in this section about divorce, swearing, and an eye for an eye and what he later taught about eating "unclean" foods and observing the Sabbath (all of which are part of the Law of Moses), it's obvious that the teachings he talked about in these two verses must apply only prior to accepting the fulfillment Jesus brought. However, the fulfillment Jesus taught does fulfill the real intent of the Law of Moses—thus providing a true fulfillment.

[3] Good News 9:28-33 (Matthew 5:17-20).

[4] Good News 9:69 (Matthew 5:48). This verse is often translated as if Jesus commanded his followers to be as perfect as God, but that's not really what Jesus did. In the language of the New Testament, the word translated "perfect" is also translated "mature" or "full grown." Jesus never commanded his followers to do what is truly impossible.

What Jesus was demanding of his followers was that they must grow and mature toward the spiritual maturity they would find in God. In other words, he was saying that we need to focus our lives on God—which is the very definition of Christian faith or belief that we've been talking about. It's ending the rebellion. We as Christians are to find our motivation in focusing our lives on God and on doing his will in this world—knowing that his will is forgiving, caring, unselfish, generous, active love toward him and toward each other. We're to make God's will our motivation—and doing so will always reinforce that motivation because of the rewards of peace, joy, and God's own Holy Spirit within (always provided to his followers), regardless of external circumstances. When we're willing to make this the focus of our lives, however imperfectly we live out that focus, God enters the picture with the grace to cover every failure.

Points to Consider:
1. Seriously consider the idea of "Love God and do what you want" or "do your best for God and let God deal with the rest." How do you react to that idea?
2. Seriously consider the problems with law mentioned in this section. Can you think of specific examples in your life where you have felt justified to get around the law?
3. Seriously consider Jesus' words about fulfilling the law as seen in what he said right after that. (Read the passage.) Can you see the truth of the idea that the fulfillment Jesus was talking about actually did away with the law as law?
4. Seriously consider Jesus' conclusion to his discussion of the law where he talked about maturity. Does that make sense to you in light of all that Jesus said in that passage?

FAITH VERSUS LAW FOR CHRISTIANS

At this point, because of all the misunderstanding among Christians about the role of works vs. faith and grace and because of the very common practice of some trying to turn Christianity into a set of rules and laws, we need to return to the subject of law versus faith in Christianity. When we're children or immature, we need rules to control our behavior. When the focus of our lives is selfishness and worldly interests, we're spiritual infants and we need earthly laws to control our behavior. But when we live by the kind of faith presented in the Bible, laws become unnecessary. In fact, for people who have this kind of faith in God, laws tend to actually weaken faith.

Paul strongly emphasized that justification (and therefore salvation) is a direct function of faith, and that living by rules and laws cannot do what faith does[5]. One of his strongest points is that if justification were by obeying God's Law (the Ten Commandments and other related Old Testament laws), those who succeeded in obeying the law would have reason to boast about what they'd accomplished, but since it's by faith (focusing one's life on God and trusting God to save), no one has anything to boast about. Faith is turning your life over to God and trusting him to rescue you. It's like grabbing the rescue harness extended from the rescue helicopter and leaving any flotation device behind. You may say that you have faith in the harness and the helicopter, but until you actually grab the harness and put it on, you can't be rescued.

Later in his letter to the Roman Christians Paul said,

> What are we saying, then? Should we just keep on sinning because we aren't under laws and rules since our sins are all covered by God's grace? May that thought never have existence! Don't you know that you're actually the slaves of whomever you choose to obey? So if you choose to obey sin, that obedience will lead to death. But if you choose to obey righteousness, that obedience will lead to life everlasting[6].

Paul was making it clear that the faith he talked about couldn't be compatible with living by our fleshly desires while insisting that we're still not subject to any laws or rules. God's plan works very well as long as we keep our lives focused on living for him and living in caring love, but as soon as we decide to turn our backs on that and go our own way, we voluntarily and intentionally put ourselves outside of God's plan.

---

[5] See Romans 3:20-30 and the entire book of Galatians.
[6] Romans 6:15-16.

Saving faith necessarily leads to obedience, but not legalistic obedience—rather, obedience of the heart. A person who doesn't focus his or her life on living for God doesn't have saving faith and doesn't really love God. How successful this focusing will be is an individual thing, and God knows how to judge whether a person has actually focused his or her life on him or whether that person has only made a show of doing so. Hopefully you can see the link here to the prophecies of Jeremiah about a new covenant of the heart[7].

Notice how Paul contrasts law and grace in the passage in Romans 6, we aren't under law but under grace. The point here is the very ability of God's Law to have enforcement. If we're under grace, there's no penalty for breaking a law, because any infraction is immediately covered by that grace. The force of any law is the penalty for breaking that law. For the Christian, there's no penalty, so the law has no power. The point that Paul is making and that we must understand is that if we focus our lives on our worldly selves or on the things of this world (including living up to some legal standard), we aren't Christians, and therefore we aren't under grace. But if we focus our lives on living for God, the law becomes an informative guide to help us understand what that should mean, but it has no hold on us when we fall short.

In writing to the Christian teams in Galatia Paul said, "Therefore the Law of Moses was our guide to bring us to Christ, so that we could be justified by faith[8]." In this passage the word "guide" (sometimes translated "tutor" or "schoolmaster") didn't mean a formal teacher. Paul used the word for a slave whose duty it was to escort a child to and from a place of learning. This slave did provide instruction and guidance in general areas of life as he would lead the child to and from school, but he wasn't the child's true teacher. So the law functioned in the role of this slave, bringing us safely to where we could focus our lives on God, who is our true teacher. From the law we gain insight into what God wants from his people, just as the child gained general insights for living from his "tutor." But the real instructor is God, not the Law.

Later in that same letter Paul was discussing the fact that some whom he'd led to Christ were being misled by others to practice circumcision as a legalistic requirement imposed on any who would be Christians. Circumcision wasn't one of the Ten Commandments, but it was a small part of the Law of Moses. Speaking of this or any other part of that law, Paul said, "Those of you who want to be justified by keeping rules have cut yourselves off from Christ—you've fallen away from God's grace[9]." In other words, if we try to gain favor with God by earning his admiration through obedience to one or more laws or rules, we cease to even be Christians. God's role is paying the price of our sins, and when we try to take over God's role, we shut God out.

But to make it clear that Christians are by definition focused on living for God, Paul told the Christian teams in Galatia,

> Don't let anyone fool you. You cannot make a mockery of God. Whatever a person sows is exactly what that person will reap. The one who sows selfishness and worldliness shall reap corruption along with those worldly things, but the one who sows for a spiritual harvest will, from the Holy Spirit, reap everlasting life[10].

To the Christians in Corinth Paul wrote, "Everything is lawful for me, but some things aren't helpful. Everything is lawful for me, but I won't be brought under the power of any[11]," and then again "Everything is lawful for me, but some things aren't helpful, everything is lawful for me, but some things aren't useful in building the kingdom[12]." Paul was always insistent that nothing in God's Law applies to Christians as law because God's grace would immediately cover any violation.

But that didn't mean Christians could focus on selfish desires and worldly things and still be Christians. As soon as a person turns his or her back on God to focus on self, that person turns from Christianity and has fallen from grace.

---

[7] Jeremiah 31:31-34.
[8] Galatians 3:24.
[9] Galatians 5:4.
[10] Galatians 6:7-8.
[11] 1Corinthians 6:12.
[12] 1Corinthians 10:23.

It should be obvious how these teachings are compatible with faith or belief as a focus of one's life on God, and with no other definition.

Please don't misunderstand this. Falling from grace isn't a simple slip or a deviation from your normal focus on God; it requires an intentional turning your back on God[13]—actual apostasy. To be guilty of this, a person must first have come to experience God's presence through his Holy Spirit and to have experienced the awesome blessings of Christianity. Only God can judge when a person has done this, and once a person truly experiences God in his or her life the risk of such apostasy is extremely low, but the door is never closed.

James wrote

> If you really fulfill the royal law according to the Scripture, 'You shall love your neighbor as yourself,' you do well, but if you show partiality, you're sinning, and are convicted by that same law as transgressors. For anyone who keeps the whole law and yet stumbles in one point, he's guilty of all[14].

Remember, "You shall love your neighbor as yourself[15]" was part of the Law of Moses. Since this is true, it should be obvious that no one could possibly live a good enough life to earn salvation.

Hopefully it's clear to anyone who can understand these passages that James, Paul, Jesus, and whoever wrote Hebrews are all in agreement about this—Christians are those who focus their lives on and find their motivation in God and his supreme commandment to love each other with an caring, unselfish, generous, forgiving, active love—something that can never be fulfilled as law. Those who don't have such a focus but are instead motivated by the things of this world are just not Christians and are therefore condemned under God's Law as delivered to Moses. And those who try to deserve or earn salvation by keeping laws and rules have no hope, because they are actually trying to take over God's job.

Points to Consider:
1. Seriously consider how you perceive the biblical message about law versus grace and faith versus works. If your perspective doesn't match the one in this section of the study, provide biblical evidence to support your view.
2. Seriously consider again the concept of faith as focusing your life on living for God. Do you think that is the biblical perspective? If not, what biblical evidence can you suggest that would disagree with it?
3. Trying to think from God's perspective, does this concept of faith as focusing your life on living for God seem reasonable?

Summary Questions:
1. Did this section help you in any way, and if so, how? Be specific.

2. What do you see as the most important point or points of this section when it comes to Christians being motivated?

3. Jot down a note or two about anything you learned new in studying this section or anything you understood better because of studying this section.

---

[13] See Hebrews 6:4-6.
[14] James 2:8-10.
[15] Leviticus 19:18.

CHRISTIANITY 102 – FAITH—THE ULTIMATE FOCUS - PART 3

REVISITING POPULAR NEW TESTAMENT PASSAGES

Now that we know that "faith" and "belief" are the same thing in the New Testament and we know that the meaning of Christian faith or belief involves focusing one's life on living for God, let's consider how this changes our understanding of two familiar New Testament passages.

John 3:16 says, "For God so loved the world that he gave his only begotten Son, that whoever believes in him should not perish but have everlasting life (NKJV)." With the understanding we've just gained, it would be entirely legitimate to do an amplified translation that said, "You see, this shows how very much God cared for the world in that he gave[1] his unique son so that anyone entrusting his or her life to Jesus would escape destruction and have life forevermore[2]." That translates the concept expressed by the apostle John into English, and that's certainly consistent with what Jesus always taught.

In Acts 16, Paul and Silas had just been freed from jail (along with other prisoners) by an earthquake. The jailer knew that if his prisoners escaped, he would be subject to the punishment due each escaped prisoner, and he was preparing to kill himself to avoid that punishment and the shame his family would experience when Paul called out to let him know that none of the prisoners had fled. The jailer must have been somewhat familiar with what Paul had been teaching before he was imprisoned, because he called out to Paul, "What must I do to be saved?" Paul told the jailer, "Believe on the Lord Jesus Christ, and you'll be saved, you and your household[3]." Now, to properly understand what Paul said, we need to apply what we've just learned.

Again, an amplified version that translates the ideas as Paul meant them and as the jailer would have understood them might well read, "Make the Lord Jesus and his will the focus of your life, and you'll be saved—you and anyone in your household who does the same." If we understand this, then the point Paul was making supports what Jesus taught exactly. Many other well-known passages need to be revisited in a similar way. The issue is, indeed, lordship. When Paul said "Believe in the Lord Jesus," he wasn't using the word "Lord" lightly.

Points to Consider:
1. Seriously consider the meaning of John 3:16 in light of what you've learned in this study. Can you think of practical application of this meaning?
2. Seriously consider Paul's words to the jailer in Philippi. How does the concept we're learning here affect they normal understanding of this passage?
3. Considering Paul's use of the word "Lord," what do you think the jailer would have understood from Paul's words?

Biblical View

For some people, this won't be what you've heard most of your life, and it may be hard to accept this different perspective. If that's the case for you, please take the time to study this material carefully. We need to put the message of the Bible ahead of the message of traditions, no matter how long those traditions have been taught. Remember, there's not much Jesus condemned more firmly than the fact that the Pharisees of his day had allowed their traditions to take the place of God's message.

In the passages just reviewed and many other passages, we see that Jesus, James, Paul, and Christians of that period in general all agreed that Christian faith, if it's to be saving faith, must motivate how we live. For those who've truly come to know the Lord, this should be no surprise. God demands that we end the rebellion; he's always demanded our hearts, a motivated focus on doing his will.

"Give me your heart," says the Father above,

---

[1] The tense of the verb indicates that this isn't what Jesus said, but what John wrote about something that had already happened.
[2] Good News 15:24.
[3] Acts 16:30-31 (NKJV).

No gift so precious to him as our love.
From this dark world he would call you apart,
Speaking so earnestly, "Give me your heart[4]."

God knows that we'll experience many failures in our efforts to serve him, but he insists that we must try. That's the message of the first chapters of Genesis, and that's the core message of the Revelation and everything in between. As we saw earlier, Paul emphasized that we belong to the one we serve as slaves—whether we serve God or Satan. In fact, the whole New Testament makes it abundantly clear that Christianity and salvation are a matter of accepting God's divine authority over our lives. **The rebellion must end**.

Now in saying that the rebellion must end, we aren't saying that a Christian must stop sinning and live a perfect life. In this world, God knows that we can't completely stop sinning no matter how hard we try. Until he pulls us out of the riptide of sin that permeates this world, we won't have the ability to overcome sin completely. What God does demand is that we shift the focus of our lives from living for ourselves and our own pleasures to living for him. He knows the changes we can accomplish will be limited. He knows that we'll need his forgiveness over and over. He only asks that we honestly and sincerely try to turn our lives around and trust his guidance. And what he asks us to try to learn to do is all good—caring love, faithfulness, doing the right thing, caring for others, being truthful, seeking peace, forgiving others as he's forgiven us, and the list of these good things goes on with everything motivated by the first thing on the list—caring love.

To be honest, it's often difficult to determine today what Christians of the New Testament period might have understood as the meaning of a particular word or phrase, especially if that word or phrase isn't used much in the Bible. But from the information here, it should be obvious that Christians in New Testament times would have included the idea of focusing one's life on what one believes as the essence of Christian faith or belief. Saving faith must be faithful. Of course, 'faith' or 'belief' must also include accepting certain truths on the testimony of other Christians, that's an important part of the meaning, but that isn't the full meaning for Christians. We'd never accept God's authority over our lives if we didn't believe "that he exists and that he rewards those who sincerely seek him[5]," but we must not overlook that Christian faith isn't just believing that God exists—an important factor of Christian faith is to "sincerely seek" God's will for one's life.

Points to Consider:
1. Seriously consider the difference between ending the rebellion and being perfectly sinless. Does this make sense to you?
2. Seriously consider ideas about what God would consider "good enough." Do you think God's standard might be different for different people based on their abilities, their environment, or their background?

THE ALTERNATIVE DEFINITION FOR 'FAITH' OR 'BELIEF'

Now let's consider the alternative to this definition for faith or belief. Assume for this moment that the word 'belief' or 'believe' in the Bible applies only to certain truths we must believe.

This actually results in an impossibly difficult situation that's effectively a form of works salvation. The question becomes, "What must we believe?" If we go by Paul's answer to a jailer in Philippi ("Believe in the Lord Jesus, and you'll be saved[6]") then we must believe in Jesus. But what must we believe about him—that he was born? That he was born of a virgin? That he was God's son? That he was God in the flesh? That he was crucified for our sins? That he rose from the dead? That he ascended to heaven? Is it necessary to believe in Jesus' miracles? Where is the dividing line between what's enough and what's not enough, and who establishes that line?

---

[4] Adapted from the hymn "Give Me Thy Heart" by Eliza Hewitt, 1898, in the public domain.
[5] Hebrews 11:6.
[6] Acts 16:31.

Paul wrote that belief in the resurrection is necessary[7]. Hebrews tells us that we must believe that God exists and that he rewards those who seek him[8]. Jesus said that people should believe the gospel—that is, the good news[9].

What do these passages all mean? What should we include as part of the gospel? Must a person search the whole Bible looking for this or that passage that adds something we must believe? (And of what use can it be to say that we believe the whole Bible when we know little if anything about what the Bible says?)

There are also passages that tell us that people who believe certain things won't be saved. For example, the Galatian Christians were warned by Paul against believing that obeying the law of circumcision was necessary for salvation[10]. Here is a passage where one thing in the Bible tells us not to do something else in the Bible. What happens if we get this wrong and accidentally believe something that we weren't supposed to believe?

Going further, must we believe in the Genesis account of creation or a specific interpretation of that account? Must we believe in the story of Jonah's or Daniel's experiences as actual events? (I happen to believe these, but some who claim to be Christians and who seem to be serving God to the best of their abilities do not.) Must we believe in a global flood in Noah's time? Must we believe in the inerrancy of the Bible? What if we fail to believe one of these things? Or what if we believe something that isn't on God's list of things to believe? Would we be lost?

The fact is that many different Christian leaders have different lists of the things they think must be believed. If the term 'believe' involves believing certain truths, then we must find out what those truths are and believe all of them and only them. So whose list should we believe?

With this approach, we must constantly be concerned lest there be something we should have believed that we haven't believed or something we shouldn't have believed that we believed. There's no security in salvation based on such a task.

However, if the "faith" or "belief" focuses on shaping our lives around the desires of the one we believe in, then the whole issue of *what* to believe disappears. The issue isn't what we believe, but in whom we place our trust and confidence. In fact, as mentioned earlier, 'trust' and 'confidence' are alternate meanings of the New Testament word for 'belief.' In this way we aren't responsible for a list of things to believe, but rather we're responsible for living according to what we know of God's will for our lives. Since it's the belief or faith that matters, we aren't even held accountable for what we don't know—we're only accountable for what we do know and for seeking to know more. God's responsible for what he wants to reveal to us, and we can trust him to faithfully do his part as long as we remain open to his word and eager to learn.

THE EVIDENCE OF OTHER NEW TESTAMENT TERMS

When we look at certain other New Testament terms, we find a wonderful agreement with this definition of faith or belief. For example, the term 'repentance' means "to change one's mind, to change one's focus"—in other words, to stop following our own path in life and start following God's path. Repentance is a shift of life focus from self and worldly things to God and his kingdom; it's taking on a new set of motivations based on your caring love for God and your caring love for others. Just as repentance is the act of changing your mind from a focus on self and worldly things to a focus on God and spiritual things, so faith is maintaining your focus on God and spiritual things. The only way to come to saving faith is by repentance, and this kind of repentance always leads you to saving faith.

Points to Consider:
1. Seriously consider the concept of "believing in facts" as a form of earning salvation by figuring out the right set of things to believe. Does the difficulty here make sense to you?
2. Are there any things you know of that some Christians hold as necessary beliefs that other Christians consider either unnecessary or actually wrong to believe?

---

[7] Romans 10:9.
[8] Hebrews 11:6.
[9] Good News 8:17 (Mark 1:15).
[10] Galatians 5:1-4.

Picture repentance this way: A man is walking toward the edge of a cliff with a shear drop of hundreds of feet to a rocky surface below. He has no awareness of the danger. His eyes are focused on things around him, not on where his feet are going. Then he sees the danger just before falling over the edge. He immediately stops, but that isn't repentance. As long as he still faces the cliff, sooner or later he'll fall over if only because the cliff erodes. Even if he turns around to face the other direction, if he remains where he is, he'll eventually fall over. But when he turns around and starts walking the opposite direction, that's repentance, and that's when he's safe. (Faith would be like continuing to walk in this new direction.)

And certainly, the term 'kingdom of God' implies that God is king. Speaking of Jesus as Lord ought to mean that we serve him as our lord. Too many Christians speak of Jesus as Lord thinking that he's Lord of the universe and Lord of heaven and Lord of the whole creation without perceiving that he insists on being Lord of each person's life. As Jesus said,

> Not everyone who says to me, "Lord, Lord," will get into the kingdom of heaven, but only the one who does the will of my Father in heaven. On judgment day, many will say to me, "Lord, Lord, didn't we preach in your name and drive out demons and perform many miracles in your name?" Then I'll tell them, "Just get away from me, you who have no regard for God's laws, I never knew you at all[11]."

Jesus made it clear that his lordship must affect our lives, not just outwardly in what we say or in demonstrations we put on for show, but as the central core issue of life. Prophesying and doing miracles isn't the issue. Saying "Lord, Lord," isn't the issue. Living for him, making him Lord of our lives, is the issue.

In fact, the very word "Christian" means "belonging to Christ." In New Testament times, this would imply that Christ has the same authority over us that a master would have over his slave. When we say that we're Christians, we effectively say that we're slaves of Christ—bought, paid for, and owned by him. Paul wrote to the Christians in Corinth to tell them "you are not your own" because "you were bought at a price[12]."

The New Testament word for love also connects to this concept. Caring love deals with a servant love—a love that does for others. Thus if the first and greatest commandment is to love God with all one's heart, soul, mind, and body, this includes serving God. Once again, God's divine authority is central. Christianity is a lordship issue.

Points to Consider:
1. Seriously consider the comparison between biblical repentance and biblical faith as presented in this study. Does this make sense to you?
2. Seriously consider the idea of the "kingdom of God" and how that fits with the biblical concept of faith as presented in this study. Does it make sense to you that you must accept God as your king?
3. Seriously consider the concept of Jesus as Lord and how that fits with the biblical concept of faith as presented in this study. Does it make sense to you that you must accept Jesus as your Lord?
4. Seriously consider the meaning of the word "Christian" and how this applies to our understanding of faith. How do you react to the idea of being Jesus' slave?
5. Seriously consider the meaning of caring love as defined by Jesus and how that applies to understanding faith. Does it make sense that loving God as Jesus described must include seeking to do his will?
6. The point of this part of the study is that a person can't be a Christian without accepting God's authority over his or her life. Seriously consider this concept and how it compares with other, more common, views of Christianity. In what ways is this different from what others teach about Christianity?

---

[11] Good News 11:38-40 (Matthew 7:21-23).
[12] 1Corinthians 6:19-20.

JESUS' TESTIMONY

Jesus said this more than once, and it was probably an often repeated theme in his ministry: "'Indeed,' Jesus told his disciples and those standing around him, 'if you want to follow my ways, you've got to take the focus of your life off of yourself! You've got to face every day ready to be executed as a criminal just because you're my disciple—living as I've taught you[13].'" This isn't a suggestion. The words Jesus used are actually commands from the Lord. We cannot be acceptable as Jesus' followers if we aren't willing to at least try to do this, and this is the very definition of saving faith—truly putting the focus of our lives on Jesus. Saving faith is and must be faithful.

Point to Consider:
1. Seriously consider the concepts covered in this section and how these concepts should affect the daily lives of those who claim to be Christians. What are some practical things this would mean in your life?

ASSUMPTIONS CONCERNING FREE WILL IN HEAVEN

There's another point that demonstrates just how important this matter must be. It also answers many questions about God's purposes both in this creation and in the world to come. This point has to do with something Christians have come to believe with no biblical support. Many Christians believe that we lose our freedom in heaven. Many and probably most Christians today believe that once we reach heaven we'll no longer be able to sin—sin would be impossible. Yet, the Bible never says that. In fact, the Bible provides strong evidence against that idea. Not that there'll be sin in heaven (there will not), or even that we'll be tempted to sin in heaven (we will not)—but there's very good reason to understand that this will be true because those who are there would always recognize sin for what it is and would never want to go near it.

When God created this world, he created humans with the ability to choose between right and wrong. After creating the humans with this ability, God pronounced his creation to be "very good." That "very good" included his gift of free will to humans—the ability to rebel against their creator. If this was a good gift, then why would God take it away from us when he takes us to his new eternal world? If it was a bad gift, why did God ever give it to us, and how could he pronounce the creation "very good" with this in it? Furthermore, which of us would really want to be a robot, unable to choose between right and wrong?

The implication of the creation account is that having free will is an integral part of what God wants humans to be. If God changes us so drastically that we no longer have free will, he won't really have saved us—he'll have changed us into something we never were before.

And if God were going to redesign us so that we couldn't sin once we get to heaven, why not design us that way from the beginning so that sin would never be a threat? Why make us go through the experience of earth when we could have gone straight to heaven? Why would a loving God risk having most people lost when he could have avoided that risk? Why would he design a creation where his son would have to die if he were going to change that same creation into something that would never have required that death?

But love, the kind of real love that's the essence of Christianity, demands a choice. One cannot love with caring love without having a choice not to love. A robot cannot have this kind of love, because it's the very nature of caring love to be a choice, and it's the nature of a robot to be incapable of making personal choices. Thus, if there's to be love in heaven, there must be at least the ability to choose not to love. But the choice not to love, as we've already seen, is the very definition of sin—in other words, we must have the ability to rebel in order to have love, and rebellion is sin.

Love, this kind of love, is a vital factor in what will make heaven a paradise. Without such caring love, heaven cannot be the place of joy and fulfillment that it must be in order to be a paradise. And as long as caring love is necessary, the potential to sin must be equally necessary.

---

[13] Good News 35:31-32 (Luke 9:23). Most English translations say something like this: "If anyone desires to come after me, let him deny himself…" Jesus actually used a third person command, something that doesn't exist in English. The translator has a choice of keeping the third person and losing the emphasis of the command, or changing the wording to second person and keeping the command. The typical English translation keeps the third person usage, but this translation assumes the command is more important than the use of second or third person.

Points to Consider:
1. Seriously consider the idea that the freedom to choose that God gave us must make sin a possibility in heaven unless God changes us into something we're not. Does that make sense to you?
2. Seriously consider the idea that it would be ridiculous for God to create us with the ability to sin in this world if he were going to take that ability away when we get to heaven. Does that make sense to you?
3. Seriously consider the idea that the very presence of caring love in heaven must mean that we would have a choice to sin in heaven if we wanted to. Considering Jesus' definition of caring love, can you imagine a way to have that kind of love without having a choice not to love?

Summary Questions:
1. Did this section help you in any way, and if so, how? Be specific.

2. What do you see as the most important point or points of this section when it comes to Christians being motivated?

3. Jot down a note or two about anything you learned new in studying this section or anything you understood better because of studying this section.

CHRISTIANITY 102 – FAITH—THE ULTIMATE FOCUS - PART 4

AN EXTENDED ILLUSTRATION—RIPTIDE

The ability to sin doesn't mean that there'll be sin in heaven, or that we'll be in any danger of falling back into sin. Earlier we used an illustration of a man named Tom living beside the ocean who liked to use an inner tube to float in the surf. In that story, Tom got caught in a riptide without ever knowing what was happening—he felt entirely safe while he was being dragged to his doom. But when he finally realized his danger, he cried out for help. We saw how, in a similar way, people must be aware of real danger before they'll really turn to God for salvation.

Extending this same illustration, imagine that, after struggling against the riptide and finding that his condition was truly hopeless, Tom was rescued by a helicopter. The helicopter dropped a rope with a safety harness, and he was lifted out of the riptide and placed on the shore. Having now perceived the danger of riptides, and having been rescued from certain death, would Tom ever go into the water again when there's a known risk for riptides? No normal, intelligent, healthy, well-adjusted person would do that. Tom learned to watch for the riptide warnings, and he'll never again be caught in that snare.

This is a relatively good illustration of what God has done on this earth. He's given us an environment where we can become familiar with the extreme dangers of sin and with the impossibility of rescuing ourselves. While we're here on earth, we can learn just how terrible sin really is. Once we learn this lesson and make a firm commitment to God's divine authority and against sin—in other words, once we end the rebellion—God can safely forgive our sin and take us to his new world. If God were to take us to heaven before we accepted his authority over our lives and rejected our rebellion, we'd destroy the new world just like we destroyed this one.

Points to Consider:
1. Seriously consider the idea that, once we're aware of how terrible sin is and how impossible it would be to rescue ourselves from its effects, we would never in all eternity want to do anything against God's will. Does that make sense to you?
2. Can you think of earthly examples of cases where people are intentionally put through difficult circumstances before being given great rewards?

UNDERSTANDING GOD'S PLAN

This topic must go all the way back to the creation. This is the reason for the Tree of Knowledge of Good and Evil in the garden paradise. God knew that humans would sin before he even began this creation[1]. He didn't want them to sin, but he knew it was important for them to experience sin and its effects before he could safely give them eternal life. If that weren't true, he could simply have planted a garden with no Tree of Knowledge of Good and Evil. Or if that tree were somehow necessary to the creation process, God could have planted it in some inaccessible place. But Genesis tells us that the tree was "in the midst of the garden." God made it so that Adam and Eve would see the tree routinely. And the Bible tells us that the fruit of that tree looked good!

It's very likely there was nothing magical about that tree. No magic was needed in the fruit itself. God could have used anything—a line these humans weren't to cross, a rock they weren't to touch, a direction in which they weren't to point—but he used a fruit they weren't to eat. Eating that fruit was rebellion, and rebellion is sin. For Adam and Eve, this was the only rebellion possible. Before humans rebelled, they couldn't know the difference between good and evil because they'd only experienced good. Once they ate the fruit, they'd rebelled, and that very act had to give them the knowledge of good and evil—they'd done evil for the first time. They had chosen Satan's side rather than God's side, and they knew it when they did it. Satan himself made it very clear that this was a way of going against God.

In order to receive God's eternal reward, we must end that rebellion and commit our lives to God. God can forgive any sin except final rejection of his authority. He can forgive any amount of sin. However, he won't take away the freedom that makes it possible for us to love—and that same freedom makes it possible for us to sin.

---

[1] See Ephesians 1:4; 2Timothy 1:9; Titus 1:2; and 1Peter 1:20.

And since he won't take away that freedom, it's mandatory that we learn how bad sin is and that we make a life commitment for God and against sin before he takes us to our heavenly reward. **This is the essence of discipleship. The rebellion must end!** (Remember, this doesn't mean we have the impossible task of ending all sin in our lives, but God knows whether we've truly ended the rebellion and whether we're truly trying to learn to live for him.)

Points to Consider:
1. Seriously consider the idea that God knew that it was important for humans to experience sin in this world. Does that make sense to you? Can you think of any other reason for him to plant the Tree of Knowledge of Good and Evil in a prominent place in the garden?
2. Seriously consider the idea that eating this fruit was rebellion against God, choosing the side of his enemy, Satan. Does that make sense to you?
3. Seriously consider the concept of ending the rebellion while still not being able to completely stop sinning. Does that make sense to you?

Another Illustration—Golden Gate Bridge
Many people live in the San Francisco area near the Golden Gate Bridge. Thousands cross the bridge every day. Occasionally, someone climbs the bridge and jumps to his or her death. In each case, we can be certain that the one who does something like this is either not rational, not healthy, not well adjusted, or under duress.

In heaven, God will take away our past sin and our guilt and open our eyes so that we'll know, even as we're known. Those who reach heaven will be rational, they'll be healthy, they'll be well adjusted, and they'll never be under any duress to cause them to turn against God. There'll be no Satan to tempt them. There'll be no disease or irrationality to draw them back into the sin they've escaped. They'll know the awesome joy of freedom from sin and guilt—a joy they will never really have experienced until they reach heaven. They'll understand how sin brought every form of pain and suffering to our world. And they'll be serving God in ways that will constantly have them rejoicing in that service.

For those who already have a commitment against sin, who've fought a losing battle against sin, who have a firm commitment to following God's will, and who've been rescued from sin, there'll be no risk that they would ever return to sin. Rebellion must be possible in heaven, but it will be unthinkable. We'll be in infinitely less risk of returning to sin than a healthy, sane, well-adjusted person who isn't under any duress would be at risk of jumping off the Golden Gate Bridge.

Points to Consider:
1. Seriously consider the idea that there'll be no sin in heaven because those who get there will have learned how terrible sin is. Does that make sense to you? Does it make sense that God would want us to experience the bad effects of sin in an environment where we could be forgiven and rescued?
2. Seriously consider the idea that no sane, healthy, well-balanced person who was not under duress would ever return to sin in all eternity—especially if Satan's not there to tempt. Does that make sense to you?

A Personal Illustration
When I was about 4 years old, my family lived in the little town of Saumonauk, Illinois. At the time my father was a smoker and I thought of smoking as some forbidden fruit that I'd probably enjoy based on how much my father seemed to enjoy it. So I was excited when I found a fresh unopened pack of cigarettes in the road in front of our house. Saumonauk was a very small town with very little traffic on our street, and the pack of cigarettes was completely unharmed. It had never even been opened. I had no matches, but I opened the pack and put my first cigarette in my mouth. This was before filters were added to cigarettes. This turned out to be two cigarettes—my first one and my last one—combined in one. At least in my memory, I spent the rest of the day trying to get that taste out of my mouth. However long I spent trying to get rid of the taste, I've never been tempted by cigarettes since then.

That's what God is doing with sin in this world. If this weren't the case, why would God have put humans in a world where sin is possible and then planted the tree of knowledge of good and evil where they would have to see it over and over? He saw that we would need to learn a lesson—that this lesson would be vitally important for our eternal happiness. This world is like our vaccination against sin.

Points to Consider:
1. Seriously consider the idea of this world as a vaccination against sin. Does that make sense to you? Why or why not?
2. Seriously consider how Christians should live if that is indeed the case. How does this fit with not being able to overcome sin in this world?
3. Can you think of any other concept that would really explain what's going on in this world?
4. Seriously consider the role of saving faith as explained in this study in light of this information. Does this help you understand why salvation must be a result of a choice to have faith in God?

THE GOOD NEWS OF FAITH AND LOVE

When we combine this kind of faith with caring love, Christians focused on doing God's will are going to be looking for opportunities to show caring love. This is obviously good news for those in need, but it's also astonishingly good news for the Christians. Anyone who's seriously experienced this will know how rewarding such activity is.

I recall as a teenager working on a mission project that involved sorting, cleaning, packaging, and organizing a huge amount of material to be shipped to missionaries. Several adults and a few teens had volunteered to work this project. We started early that day and worked hard all day. At the end of the day we were all exhausted. But as we talked, you could just sense the excitement and joy. Every person involved was experiencing overflowing joy. It was a skippity-doo-dah feeling I had never experienced before, but I've experienced it many times since.

After years of serving the Lord, I've come to realize how true Jesus' words are when he said; "There's more joy in giving than in receiving[2]." This is God's Holy Spirit in us, the actual presence of God himself, bringing joy beyond description. It's no wonder that Paul listed joy as the second of the fruits of the Spirit, just behind caring love[3]. I've worked long and hard at worldly tasks and have had a wonderful sense of accomplishment when the job was done, but never anything like the sense of joy that comes with working for the Lord. And this sense of joy is just a small foretaste of what's waiting for us in eternity.

This combination of faith and caring love also provides good news for Christianity in general and Christian teams in particular. When people see Christians living their faith and love, they look favorably on such Christians. When these same people see the joy that Christians experience in living this way, they want to be part of that joy. There's no more powerful means of winning others to the Lord. When Christians practice faith and caring love, people come to the Lord.

Now, as mentioned earlier, caring love doesn't mean that we throw money at people who come begging. It's our job to help people, and throwing money at beggars can backfire, causing beggars to become even more dependent on begging and enabling them in very bad habits. Sometimes money is needed, but generally there are other, more important needs. Jesus encourages us to "be clever as serpents and innocent as doves[4]."

There are a couple of important items to consider here. First, each local Christian team needs to seriously facilitate this kind of activity in the local community. This is how discipleship works. This is how people are won to the Lord. This is how the local community sees God's team in action and how the body of Christ demonstrates the love of Christ. This is a key factor in attracting people to the Christian team meetings.

The practical application is this: the local Christian team needs to seriously look at the local community to find where there are obvious needs. Then the local Christian team needs to get members involved in meeting those needs. The team needs to carry the love of Christ into the lives of the community.

Second, as Christians practice this kind of discipleship, they'll experience the joy of God's Holy Spirit in their lives—and those around them will see this. When people see others experiencing this kind of joy, they want

---

[2] Acts 20:35.
[3] Galatians 5:22.
[4] Good News 14:12 (Matthew 10:16).

to be part of whatever brings that kind of joy. People are drawn to the Christians when they see this kind of joy in Christians' lives. That's who God wants us to win the hearts of those around us.

Many Christian teams have mission programs in their budgets that provide funds for outreach in other countries, other states, or other areas in their state but have no assigned budget for ministry to local community needs. This is backward. Support for distant missions is biblical and good, but meeting local needs is also biblical, and biblically it's supposed to come first. Some may say that local needs are met by special offerings and special expenditures as the needs arise, but that leads to a lack of serious consideration of needs and a lack of intentional work to meet needs even before they would otherwise come to the attention of a Christian team. There's no more important focus for a Christian team than finding ways to minister to the needs of the local community[5].

Whether or not the local Christian team does intentional ministry to the needs of the local community, each Christian is called to do so. And while the ministry of Christians to the needs around them normally involves the local community, this ministry continues to apply wherever a Christian is. If Christians practiced this kind of discipleship as they travel on business or vacation, much of the work now done by missionaries would be unnecessary, freeing missionaries to do far more. If every person who claims to be Christian were to practice caring love wherever he or she went, the world would be changed dramatically!

Points to Consider:
1. Seriously consider the claim that the good feeling we get from helping others is actually the presence of God in our lives. Do you think this would apply to non-Christians as well as Christians?
2. Seriously consider what Jesus meant when he talked about being "clever as serpents." How do you think this would apply to helping those in need?
3. Seriously consider how you think a Christian team's budget should look when comparing ministries to local needs versus non-local ministries. Give reasons for your ideas.
4. Seriously consider how the world might be changed if Christians intentionally practiced caring love as they travel. Can you think of any potential problems with this concept? (There are some.)

THE SUMMARY OF FAITH AND LORDSHIP

This study of Christian faith shows why lordship is such an important concept for Christians to understand. To be a disciple is to accept Jesus as Lord, and that's what saving faith is all about. Accepting Jesus as Lord is also the concept Satan most desires to have us ignore or overlook. Satan would be satisfied to see Christians wage a winning battle against any sin as long as these Christians don't really submit to Jesus as Lord. A person can be perfectly moral and ethical without having any hope of salvation. A commitment to "family values" or "morality" or "ethics" or one's "church" and its doctrines or any other human-centered concept is worthless when it comes to salvation if it isn't accompanied by accepting God's divine authority. This is why a person must turn his or her life over to God before that person can be saved.

As the author of Hebrews said, "And without faith it's impossible to please God, because anyone who comes to him must believe that he exists and that he rewards those who sincerely seek him[6]." As mentioned earlier, that phrase, "sincerely seek," involves making him Lord. And as Peter said,

> This water [the water of Noah's flood that buoyed up the boat and saved those in the boat] also symbolizes the immersion that now saves you too—not because of washing the dirt from your body, but because you've committed yourself to a good conscience toward God[7].

The phrase, "committed yourself to a good conscience toward God," involves making him Lord. The message of the Bible is always the same—he must be Lord! **The rebellion must end!**

Too many times we neglect this point. We may have some "plan of salvation" that jumps from one passage to another to explain God's plan, as if God couldn't put his own plan together in one place. Or we may teach

---

[5] See Good News 40:26-36 (Matthew 25:31-46).
[6] Hebrews 11:6.
[7] 1Peter 3:21.

people to "only believe" with no indication that saving belief must include an end to the rebellion—a complete change in the focus of one's life. We may teach people to pray some "sinner's prayer" that isn't found anywhere in the Bible and that no one in the Bible ever practiced, and the "sinner's prayer" we use generally says nothing about Jesus being Lord. In fact, in most cases we say little if anything about accepting Jesus as Lord! That's Satan's victory! And far too few Christian teams provide serious discipleship training about what it means to be a Christian. Even when we teach Christian living, we teach it as something that Christians "should" do, not as something Christians must do if they are to be Christians at all, or we teach it as a bunch of rules instead of a change of heart that focuses on caring love. That's absolute rebellion against Jesus' clear commandment:

"Therefore, as you go throughout the world[8], proclaim the good news to everyone. Make disciples in every nation, immersing[9] them into the nature of[10] the Father and the son and the Holy Spirit, teaching them to live by all the things I've commanded you[11]." The bottom line is that those with saving faith are faithful, and those who aren't at least seriously trying to be faithful to God aren't saved. As Jesus said, "Be faithful to the day you die, and I'll give you the victor's crown of eternal life[12]".

We're in the most important battle in all eternity. It's far past time that we went on the offensive. That means training the Lord's army for spiritual battle with spiritual weapons. That means accepting Jesus as our Lord and making this the priority motivation of our lives. We sing, "Only Believe," and we miss what it means to believe. The tasks we have waiting for us in heaven involve our active participation and our free choice concerning what we'll do for the Lord. God knows he can trust those he'll take to heaven. Those he couldn't trust, he won't take to this eternal reward. Faith that focuses one's life on God is what brings us to the point that God can trust us. **The rebellion must end**! (Once again, this doesn't mean we have the impossible task of ending all sin in our lives, but God knows whether we've truly ended the rebellion and whether we're truly trying to learn to live for him.)

Now, a lot of what we've covered in this study up to now has been focused on the danger of not being saved if we don't focus our lives on God. But for the story to be complete, we need to focus next on the awesome rewards that God promises for those who do end the rebellion.

Summary Questions:
1. Did this section help you in any way, and if so, how? Be specific.

2. What do you see as the most important point or points of this section when it comes to Christians being motivated?

3. Jot down a note or two about anything you learned new in studying this section or anything you understood better because of studying this section.

---

[8] This is often translated as a command to "go," but in the Bible the word is a participle and should be translated "going," "as you go," or "wherever you go."
[9] Translating this word as "immersing" brings out how Christians are immersed into the very nature of God. It's an immersion in water, but it's also a spiritual immersion into the nature of God.
[10] Literally, "into the name of…," but with the meaning of "the nature of."
[11] Good News 52:34-35 (Matthew 28:19-20 and Mark 16:15-16) Too often Christians have focused on immersion or some other ritual with water when this Great Commission focuses on a discipleship commitment and on training. The only actual imperative verbs here are the command to proclaim the good news (from Mark 16:15) and the command to make disciples (from Matthew 28:19). There are two participles (immersing and teaching) that follow the command to make disciples, and these carry the force of that command. If you accept getting wet without accepting the responsibilities of discipleship and training, you're not a Christian—you're just a wet pagan. Remember, the word "Christian" means "slave of Christ."
[12] Revelation 2:10.

48

CHRISTIANITY 103 – HOPE—THE ULTIMATE REWARD - PART 1

If in this life only we have hoped in Christ Jesus,
we are, of all men, most to be pitied[1]

In writing to the Christians in Corinth Paul said, "Now we have these three enduring factors: faith, hope, and caring love; but the greatest of these is love[2]." Love's the first key principle of Christianity, and faith's a very close second. But hope's what keeps us going—or at least what should keep us going. In fact, hope's really the focus of Christianity that provides guidance when we don't know which way to go. As we'll learn in this chapter, the roles of love and faith must be what they are because of the hope God has prepared for us. The single most significant factor in understanding why American Christianity isn't what it should be and doesn't accomplish what it should accomplish is the terrible lack of understanding among Christians about what Christian hope really is.

Real Christian hope isn't focused on this world or anything this world has to offer. Yes, this world has some wonderful things to offer, especially in America. And right there's where we find a serious problem. We've experienced at least some of the pleasures of this world, and we've found some of those pleasures to be really good, but we haven't experienced heaven. If our concept of heaven isn't seriously better than our experience on this earth, we're almost certain to maintain a worldly focus. And people with a worldly focus can't be what Christians are supposed to be.

Heaven's the motivating factor that can and should empower our faith and our love far beyond what the threat of hell could ever do. Unfortunately, most American Christians have such a distorted concept of heaven that it provides little or no motivation. This includes most professional Christian leaders and Bible scholars, and that's a major victory for Satan.

As long as we're trying to avoid hell, we'll be severely tempted to look for the minimum commitment needed to escape. But if we're aiming for heaven, our whole perspective changes. A man in New York City with no destination in mind may be motivated to stay out of the way of traffic by standing on the sidewalk, but if he has a particular destination in mind, while he's still motivated to stay out of the traffic, he's even more motivated to reach his destination, and the sidewalk becomes a path rather than a destination.

When Jesus said that his message was "gospel"—which means "good news"—he meant it. We need to grasp that this news is and must be the most awesome, exciting, and thrilling news ever. And heaven, the real thing as taught by Jesus, is the focus of the good news—it's what makes the good news so good.

As we'll address shortly, it's much more than unfortunate that most American Christians don't view heaven as something to hope for. Indeed, most American Christians honestly dread the very thing that will take them to heaven—their own death. It probably sounds morbid now to think that we should long for our own departure from this life, but if you can grasp the things we'll cover in this chapter, you should find a very different perspective on death.

Points to Consider:
1. Seriously consider people's views of heaven. What factors you know about are most motivating? Do you find these ideas of heaven to be better than life in this world?
2. Seriously consider things in this world that you believe you'll lose once you get to heaven. How do those losses affect your desire to go to heaven?
3. Seriously consider the relative values of heaven and hell in motivating Christians. Which one do you see as more important in motivating most Christians today? Which one has been most important in motivating you up to now? If you knew for certain that there was no hell, would you be a Christian? If so, why?
4. Seriously consider people's attitudes toward death. Do the Christians you know have a good outlook on death?
5. Seriously consider how a person's concept of Christianity can affect his or her view of death. In what ways do you think a truly wonderful concept of heaven could affect a person's view of death?

---

[1] 1Corinthians 15:19.
[2] 1Corinthians 13:13.

6. Seriously consider how a person's concept of Christianity can affect his or her life. If a person saw heaven as truly a wonderful thing to be desired more than anything else, how might that affect his or her life?

THE BAD NEWS

At this point we need to emphasize that Jesus came to bring good news, but in order to understand the good news, first we need to understand the bad news against which the good news can be compared. Any news is good only in comparison to news that's not as good. Therefore, in earlier parts of this study we've looked at sin: how pervasive it is, how deeply ensnared each of us is in our rebellion against God, how justified God's wrath is against those responsible for what Jesus had to endure, and how impossible it would be for anyone to compensate in any way for his or her own sin. All of us are hopelessly entangled in sin—in a rebellion against God that makes us accessories to the murder of God's Messiah and every other murder on earth since we first began to sin. All of us are completely dependent on God's grace and forgiveness to save us from certain damnation.

Our normal view of sin is reminiscent of Jesus' story of the man trying to remove a speck from another person's eye while he had a log in his own eye[3]. We see others as the sinners while overlooking the mass of sin in our own lives. Jesus wants us to see the bad news, the logs in our own eyes.

And in these times we rarely hear a message about hell. It's as if hell has disappeared. But hell's there, and it's very real. Hell is terrible beyond the capability of human language to describe. The word Jesus used for hell was actually the name of a valley just outside the city of Jerusalem where the city's garbage was dumped. In this valley the garbage of the city burned 24 hours a day every day. The stench was terrible. The message was this: if you don't end the rebellion, you become a waste product of this creation, suitable only for the fire.

Another term for hell used in the Revelation is the "bottomless pit." I learned a little about what this might mean in 1994 when I experienced a medical test call an ENG. In a room of absolute darkness, this test induces extreme vertigo. The feeling is as of falling with no way to stop the fall. It's absolute panic. I had the test in the early afternoon, and by evening I was still so shaken that I needed a cane to walk.

I don't believe we should just scare people into becoming Christians and consider the job done—the motivational effect ends as soon as they believe they're safe. But neither do I believe that we should fail to warn people of this very real danger. Those who end the rebellion will be a welcome part of a wonderful eternity; those who don't will be rejected as good only for the garbage dump of hell. There's no intermediate purgatory where people can somehow earn the salvation they didn't accept on earth. This is our one and only chance. And I don't know what ever gave people the idea that pain and suffering could somehow pay for our sins—no amount of pain or suffering can compensate for even one rebellious act.

Once we grasp that we're damned without God's forgiveness, lost in a riptide of sin and rebellion, we should be motivated to cry out for rescue. It's at that point that God says, "All you have to do is focus your life [faith] on me and my will [caring love], and I'll forgive your sins and take the threat of hell off the table."

It's at that point that Satan tries to get us to look for an easier way out. Trust me; there's no easier way out. God wants your life focused on him—nothing less will do. You owe him that because he's your creator—not to mention what he's done to forgive your rebellion. You owe him your life all over again because of his forgiveness and grace.

Points to Consider:
1. Seriously consider the idea that, in order to have good news, there must be something that's less good. Does that make sense to you? Can you imagine something being good news without anything being less "good?"
2. Seriously consider the concept that our sin makes us accessories to the murder of God's Messiah. Does that make sense to you?
3. Seriously consider your thoughts on the reality of hell. Do you think God will actually judge people and send some who don't end their rebellion to a garbage dump called hell?
4. Seriously consider the idea that Satan would want people to look for the minimum necessary to avoid hell. Why do you think Satan might want that?

---

[3] Good News 11:3-4 (Matthew 7:3-5).

THE GOOD NEWS?

Now that we've looked briefly at the bad news, we can turn to our hope as Christians—the very best of the good news that Jesus brought: the good news of heaven. Of all the good news Jesus brought us, this is the ultimate in good news. God's intention is that this motivating factor would provide Christians with the reason to overcome all obstacles and to bear any cost in serving him.

Yet, as mentioned earlier in this study, for most Christians, their concept of heaven couldn't be described as awesome, exciting, or thrilling. In fact, given a choice between heaven and hell, Christians will choose heaven, but given a choice between heaven and earth, most American Christians choose earth with almost no exceptions.

This is evident in several areas. While there are exceptions, most Christians view death as a tragedy. If someone dies, especially at a young age, most Christians will openly say something about how tragic that death is for the person who died. We couldn't make it any clearer that we don't believe what Jesus told us about heaven. In spite of Paul's instruction to the contrary, we mourn as those who have no hope[4]. The testimony we give to the world is that we don't believe that the gospel really is good news. We don't believe that heaven's something we should anticipate with joy.

(Just so there's no misunderstanding, it's not wrong for a Christian to mourn the loss of a loved one—in fact it's very right. What's wrong is mourning as if there were no heaven or as if heaven were a loss rather than a gain.)

Points to Consider:
1. Seriously consider to what degree Christians are generally motivated by a desire to go to heaven. How do you think that might affect Christianity?
2. Seriously consider again typical concepts of what is and what is not in heaven. Seriously consider some things that might be wrong in these typical concepts. What aspects of heaven seem really wonderful to you? What aspects of heaven don't seem so wonderful to you?
3. Seriously consider Christians and mourning. What do you think should be the difference between a Christian mourning and a non-Christian mourning?

PERSPECTIVES ON HEAVEN

In part, Christians mourning as if they had no hope is caused by the fact that most Christians have a terrible concept of heaven. Examine our songs or listen to our sermons and you'll find a belief that heaven involves worshipping God forever and forever—that, and not much else.

Maybe we think that we'll worship God for all eternity, telling him over and over again how wonderful he is because of what he did back in the good old days on earth. In this concept we may be organized into angelic choirs in order to sing God's praises.

Maybe we think that we'll spend eternity tending gardens or talking about the good times we used to have on earth. Perhaps this is OK for serious gardeners, but a lot of us aren't serious gardeners.

In our worst concepts, we may float on clouds wearing scratchy woolen robes and playing golden harps (clunk, clunk). Perhaps we'll have wings, but we'll have nowhere to fly.

In the 1996 movie *The Preacher's Wife*, Denzel Washington played the part of an angel sent to earth to help a struggling preacher rekindle his faith. In this movie, the angel tells the preacher that in heaven there's this very long line of angels all eager and just waiting to get a chance to go back to earth on some mission. When the angel arrives back on earth, he's clearly overjoyed to experience again the pleasures of life on earth. The implication is that the best thing heaven has to offer is a chance to go back to earth. In other words, heaven may be OK, but earth's far, far better. If that's really the case, then God's a liar—but that's not the case!

I don't know about you or anyone else, but for me, about three months of doing nothing but telling God what a good God he is for what he did in the past on earth would turn into torment. I'd be bored out of my mind. If I faced an eternity of such boredom, I might well decide that hell could be no worse.

With such a "reward," who needs punishment? And what about those who don't enjoy singing? What about the tone deaf?

---

[4] 1Thessalonians 4:13.

Are we doomed to spend eternity in scratchy robes with golden harps going over and over whatever ways we can come up with to tell God what a great guy he is? Is God a narcissist, in love with himself? Is he a sycophant, only interested in having servants to tell him how great he is? Is he suffering from a raging inferiority complex that led him to create billions of people in hopes of finding some who would be willing to spend eternity telling him how great he is? (That may be your picture of God, but that's definitely not the God I know.)

In fact, many of our perspectives on heaven imply that God's either stupid or very cruel, because he created an entire universe including a world specially designed for people, he made sure these people could rebel against him knowing that they would rebel, he paid a terrible price for their rebellion and will still have to send most of the people he created to hell, and he has no plan to do anything with the people he's saved except to put them on a very ornate shelf for all eternity. This would be like a company sending an employee to all kinds of schools and training sessions and then assigning the employee a job of just sitting in a nice corner office with nothing to do. Worse yet, it would be like that same company taking all employees who failed to learn from these courses and killing them for their failure, even though the company has no plans to do anything with the training.

Points to Consider:
1. Seriously consider things you see as wrong with the description given here of people's ideas about heaven. Do you have ideas of heaven that are significantly better than these?
2. Seriously consider what you think might have caused the producers of the movie described here to present such a negative picture of heaven. Do you think that many Christians may have an equally negative view of heaven?
3. Seriously consider what you see as wrong with the picture of what God has done as given in the last paragraph above. Do you have a concept of eternity that avoids this scenario?

WHAT WE SAY

If you think this isn't a problem, just listen to what Christians say, and think what this communicates about our hope. I've heard Christians say all of the following and many more like these:

"Every day above ground is a good day."

"I'm still breathing, and that certainly beats the alternative."

"It's so tragic when a young person dies like that" (when said of a Christian or a child who never had the chance to understand about rebellion).

"Of course I want to go to heaven; I just don't want to go until I have to."

"I'm trying to stay alive as long as I can." (At the time I wrote this, I had just heard a variation of this from an internationally known preacher.)

Points to Consider:
1. Seriously consider things you've heard Christians say that clearly imply that their hope is not focused on heaven. Pay attention and see how many such things you can hear.
2. Seriously consider how Christians saying these things might affect non-Christians. What affect do you think these things might have on non-Christians?

THE WORLD'S RESPONSE

It's no wonder non-Christians would be turned off by our message. Who would want to become a Christians if even Christians don't want heaven except as a last resort? Who would want to become a Christian if the reward's eternal boredom? Maybe hell's worse, but how much worse can it be? Why not enjoy earth's enticements and take your chances with these two versions of eternal torment?

Let's hear what a person who's not a Christian might say.

On one hand, I hear the message of Christians, but the heaven they offer doesn't seem very enticing. And these Christians disagree with each other about what it takes to get into their heaven. Some of them say that God would never send anyone to hell because he's too loving for that. If they're right, then there's nothing to fear. Others argue that a person has to believe in God in order to avoid hell. Well, I believe there probably is some sort of God, but I don't see much difference between the different religions. All of them seem to have both some very nice members and some members who are terrorists. Why should I pick one over any of the others? How would I know I'd picked the right one? No matter what choice I make, it looks like my chances are no better than a throw of the dice, so why not just do what gives me pleasure now and not worry about what I can't resolve?

That's not an unreasonable approach for a person who only hears the normal message of Christianity. If we hope to win the world to Christianity—if we really believe that it's important to do that, then we need to renew our understanding of the message that motivated such people to choose the Lord and die for him.

Points to Consider:
1. Seriously consider how you might answer the objections of a non-Christian as given here. Do you have answers that you think would convince a person to become a Christian?
2. Seriously consider whether such issues ever bother you. If not, why not?

THE DISCIPLES OF JESUS
From the testimony of the Bible itself, those who followed Jesus and became his closest disciples were just the kind of people who might have had such views about their religion. Matthew was a tax collector—viewed as a traitor to his nation and his religion. When Peter first experienced the miraculous power of Jesus, his response was, "Oh Lord, get away from me! I'm just a sinful man![5] " and apparently James and John had a similar reaction. These men were fishermen. They weren't religious scholars, and they tended to talk like fishermen. Even after being with Jesus throughout his ministry, as Jesus was on trial for his life, the Bible tells us that Peter cursed and swore as he denied knowing Jesus[6]. Clearly, he was no stranger to profanity.

These men weren't raging heathens, but neither were they Sunday school kids or holier-than-thou. Whatever they were, somehow the message Jesus brought turned their lives around. Peter's tirade when he denied Jesus was the last gasp of the old Peter. Once these men realized that Jesus is all that he claims to be, that his message is true, there was nothing that could shake their faith in him. We need to rediscover that message.

Getting back to our present perspective on heaven, on various occasions I've asked people in a Sunday school class to mark a secret poll showing whether they would rather go to heaven soon or stay on earth as long as possible. The result's generally unanimous. No one wants to go to heaven. Yet heaven's supposed to be God's primary motivation for Christians. Paul said, "If in this life only we have hoped in Christ Jesus, we're, of all men, most to be pitied[7]." Somehow, we've lost something very, very important—the real motivation of Christianity.

Points to Consider:
1. Seriously consider your concept of Jesus' disciples compared to the concept presented here and compared to the frequent view of these men as special "saints." Do you think of Jesus' disciples as especially good men?
2. Seriously consider how you might have responded to the secret poll mentioned in the final paragraph above. Do you think this is a symptom of having lost something important about Christianity?

Summary Questions:
1. Did this section help you in any way, and if so, how? Be specific.

2. What do you see as the most important point or points of this section when it comes to Christians being motivated?

---

[5] Good News 8:29 (Luke 5:8).
[6] Good News 47:26 (Mark 14:71).
[7] 1Corinthians 15:19.

3. Jot down a note or two about anything you learned new in studying this section or anything you understood better because of studying this section.

CHRISTIANITY 103 – HOPE—THE ULTIMATE REWARD - PART 2

THE REVISED GOOD NEWS

Well, the good news is that the typical concept of heaven is wrong. (Again, if it weren't wrong, Jesus would be a liar to call his message 'good news.')

NEW EARTH AND SKY

In order to start getting a better idea of what heaven really is, we need to take a close look at some biblical teachings. As we do this, it's important to remember that the people who wrote these things were trying to put into human terms something that's completely beyond human language.

First, let's consider some of the simpler things. We won't float on clouds for all eternity. That idea probably comes from misunderstanding a few things in the Bible:

1. The word "heaven" in the Bible isn't a very specific word. (In fact, this word appears in both singular and plural forms and in both masculine and feminine forms when it's often not obvious why these changes occur.) The ancient concept of heaven is more a concept of "up there" in a very general sense. It included the air (as in "birds of the heavens[1]"); the universe of stars (as in "stars of heaven[2]"; the abode of God[3]; and the reward of God's faithful[4]. In other words, the definition of this word would include the atmosphere, the universe, outer space, and even clouds as possible definitions of "heaven." But none of those is the right definition for God's eternity.

2. Jesus described his second coming with words used hundreds of years earlier by the prophet Daniel, "People all over earth will be in anguish as they see me returning on the clouds of the sky, coming with awesome power and brilliant glory[5]." After his arrest, Jesus repeated a very similar statement to the high priest: "The time's coming when you'll see me sitting as a human[6] at the right hand of the power of God and coming in clouds of the sky[7]." This could be understood to mean that the clouds were the heaven from which Jesus would come, but it's actually more easily understood as simply saying that Jesus would come from "up there" and his coming would appear in the skies in such a way that all would see and recognize his true nature. (With our concept of a global earth, this may seem difficult for us to understand. After all, how can he appear at the same time to those on opposite sides of the earth? But for God. That isn't even a problem.)

3. When Jesus ascended into heaven, the Bible says that "he was taken up into the sky as they watched, and finally a cloud blocked their view of him[8];" and then two men in white (apparently two of God's agents) appeared and said, "Why are you standing here gazing into the sky. This Jesus, who's been taken up into the sky, will come back in much the same way as you saw him go[9]."

4. Paul wrote that we as Christians will be "caught up" to meet the Lord and Christians who've died before us "in the clouds[10]."

In all of this there's nothing that says that the "heaven" that's the reward of Christians is the same as the "heaven" of clouds in the atmosphere. As we'll soon see in Jesus' teaching, we definitely won't float on clouds for eternity.

I'd read the Revelation several times before I noticed something that was important to me: John mentions the mountains in God's new earth. John also mentions a river and a sea that sparkles like diamonds[11] because of the

---

[1] For example, see Psalm 79:2.

[2] For example, see Mark 13:25.

[3] For example, see Genesis 24:7.

[4] For example, see Matthew 5:12.

[5] Good News 41:31 (Matthew 24:30), see Daniel 7:13.

[6] Literally, "the son of man sitting…"

[7] Good News 47:19 (Matthew 26:64).

[8] Good News 53:10 (Acts 1:9).

[9] Good News 53:12 (Acts 1:11).

[10] 1Thessalonians 4:17

[11] New earth = Revelation 21:10; River = Revelation 22:1; Sparkling sea = Revelation 4:6.

purity of the water. He mentions trees that grow along the banks of the river. In other words, John describes a beautiful world with high mountains, beautiful rivers, and an ocean of clean, clear water. God created us for a world, and he'll give us a new world—a better one undamaged by sin.

Beyond this, we still need to be careful what conclusions we draw from what the Bible does tell us. For example, the Bible mentions that there'll be no night in heaven. The fact that there'll be no night doesn't mean that God won't provide a way for us to enjoy the beauty of a night sky. John was telling us that the aspects of evil will no longer have darkness to hide in, and we'll no longer need to stumble in the dark or fear what's in the dark as we enjoy the beauty of that night sky. Even in this world, the night sky's always there—the light of the sun just blinds us to its beauty. In God's new world I expect we'll be able to see that beauty whenever we want to. I also expect that our vision capabilities in that world will allow us to see things we've never been able to see in this creation. After all, the message is that this reward will be better than, not less than, this world.

Similarly, the colors of sunrise and sunset are always there in this world, but the brightness of the day and the darkness of the night hide the colors. In God's new world, I believe we'll always be able to see those colors whenever we want to. And I expect that we'll be able to see colors that are invisible to us in this world. In high school, most of you probably studied something called the electro-magnetic spectrum. If you remember anything about that, you may recall that one very small portion of that spectrum is visible light. Biologists tell us that some portions of the spectrum that are entirely invisible to us are visible to certain other animals. Have you ever wondered how much more beautiful the universe might be if we could see those other "colors"?

In other words, I'm convinced that the God who created this beautiful world won't give us a far less beautiful world—I believe firmly that he'll give us a far more beautiful world, and I further believe that he'll enhance our ability to experience that beauty.

There's an important principle here that's clearly implied in the Bible. Heaven will be far, far better than this world. If something is good in this world, then either that same thing will be in heaven or something similar but much better. When we get to heaven, God isn't going to deprive us of the joys we've found in this world.

But having a beautiful perfect world with towering mountains, sparkling seas, fruitful trees, and colors beyond imagination is hardly even the beginning. If that were all, we'd eventually tire of heaven.

Points to Consider:
1. Seriously consider the world's view of heaven as fluffy clouds as opposed to the picture of mountains, rivers, seas, and trees presented in the Revelation. What was your image of heaven before reading this? Does the biblical image seem better than what you had previously imagined?
2. Suggest things you can think of that could be better in heaven. Think about the five senses.
3. Seriously consider things that people sometimes think will not be present in heaven. Does this perspective give you a different view?
4. Seriously consider things you enjoy or think you would enjoy in this world. Are there any of these things that would not be in heaven, and if so, why not? Even for those things that you enjoy but that won't be in heaven, do you think God could provide something just as good or better? See what you can come up with.
5. Seriously consider how God's caring love for us might affect what we experience in heaven. In what ways could this help us understand what will and what won't be in heaven?

POUNDS AND TALENTS

Have you ever had absolutely nothing to do? Perhaps you were in a hospital or confined to your bed at home. Perhaps you were in an office with all your tasks completed, but unable to leave. Perhaps you were in a prison. Whatever the case, those who've had that experience know that there are few things worse than having long hours of nothing to do. Boredom can quickly become torment.

In light of this, one very important insight about eternity comes from a story Jesus told, but before I can share this, it's important to understand that Jesus never told more of a story than what was needed to communicate the lesson or lessons he wanted to convey. When he'd told enough of the story to make the point or points he wanted, he stopped. Some of his stories are only one sentence long.

Given this truth, we'll now look at a story Jesus told twice with some minor changes in the details. (Like any good teacher, Jesus certainly would have used similar stories in different settings, changing some details to suit the particular setting.) This story involves money, and one of the details Jesus changed was the value of the money. The story is generally called by the name of the money he talked about, so in one case it's called "the story of the pounds[12] (or minas)" and in the other case it's known as "the story of the talents[13]." (In biblical times, talents were a measure of weight, and the word was often used for a weight of gold or silver.)

Each version of the story tells of a wealthy master who entrusted a lot of money to each of three slaves. In each case two of the slaves put the money to good use, and the third simply hid what he was given so that it wouldn't be at risk. In each case, the master congratulated the faithful slaves who used what he'd entrusted to them and condemned the unfaithful slave who failed to provide good stewardship of his trust. In each case the unfaithful slave lost even what he'd been given. Obviously these stories teach us multiple lessons. First, they teach us to be faithful stewards of the blessings God gives us. Second, they teach us that God's given different people different levels of stewardship, but that he expects every person to faithfully use whatever he or she's received. Third, they teach us that a failure to faithfully use what's been entrusted to us is as bad as misusing God's trust—doing nothing isn't an acceptable response to God's gifts. Fourth, they teach us that, in the end, those who don't faithfully use God's gifts will lose everything. And others may see additional lessons.

However, there's another point Jesus made in both cases that's generally overlooked. When the master commended the faithful slaves, it would've been enough in the story to have him say, "Well done, good and faithful servant. Enter into the joy of your lord." Yet Jesus intentionally added another phrase: "You've been faithful over a few things, I'll make you ruler over many things[14]." In Luke's account, the master said, "Because you've been faithful in a very little, you have authority over ten cities[15]." Though Jesus varied the details when he told this story, in each case he made the point that faithful stewards will be given greater authority and responsibility, and in the context he was applying this to heaven.

Heaven won't be eternal boredom. God has things for us to do—things we'll find great joy in doing. He knows us better than we know ourselves, and he loves us more than we can know, so the things he's prepared will be joy beyond description.

We'll look at this closer later, but I can tell you that I find greater joy in doing what God's called me to do than in anything else in this world, even though people whose lives are focused on this world would say that I received no payment at all for doing these things. I'm convinced that what we do in eternity will be that much more exciting and rewarding.

Points to Consider:
1. Seriously consider the problem of having nothing to do and how that might relate to the concept many people have of heaven. How does the concept of heaven you've had compare to this?
2. Consider the two stories mentioned here, especially the master's comment about rewarding faithfulness. Does that seem like a reasonable thing for a master to do? Do you agree that God might do something like this? Why or why not?
3. Seriously consider the idea of finding joy in serving God in this life. Do you find that to be true? Do you think we will find joy in serving God in eternity?
4. In this world, can you think of cases where people are given great rewards once they have demonstrated faithfulness in what they do?

JUDGING ANGELS
Paul made a similar point when he said,

---

[12] Good News 37:59-75 (Luke 19:12-27).
[13] Good News 37:59-75 (Matthew 25:14-30).
[14] Good News 37:65 footnote (Matthew 25:21).
[15] Good News 37:65 (Luke 19:17).

Don't you know that the saints shall judge the whole cosmos? And if you're going to judge the cosmos, are you unworthy to judge the smallest matters? Don't you know that we'll judge God's agents? How much more should we be able to judge things that pertain to this earthly life[16]?

In this case we shouldn't think of "judge" like an American judge sitting at a bench, passing sentence on those brought before him. The biblical world knew nothing of separation of powers in the government. In the biblical world, every judge was a political leader. We need to think of "judge" as in the biblical book called Judges, that is, as a leader or ruler. And the word "agent" here is often translated "angel," but this would mean an agent of God with authority—biblical "angels" are the government agents for the kingdom of God.

The message a person reading Paul's words in biblical times would have received is that at least some faithful Christians would receive positions of authority and leadership in God's eternity, and if they were to have such leadership and authority in heaven, they should be able to exercise the judgment here in this world that would be required of such leaders. The idea is that at least some Christians will be leaders of teams of God's agents. (Not everyone would enjoy that, so that's not what everyone will do. The point is not that we'll all be "judges" or leaders, the point is that we'll all be rewarded in ways that will bring us every greater joy.)

Points to Consider:
1. Seriously consider what you do know and what you may not know about biblical judges. How do the concepts mentioned here affect your understanding of what Paul wrote?
2. Seriously consider what that might mean for what God has in store for us in eternity. Can you think of things you would love to do in a new world?

THE KINGDOM
During his earthly ministry Jesus told his disciples, "I absolutely assure you, when God's rule is restored and I as a human sit on my glorious throne[17], the twelve of you who've followed me so faithfully will sit on twelve thrones exercising authority over the twelve tribes of Israel[18]." Remember Jesus' description of the judgment as separation of sheep from goats? In that passage, those who've been faithful to God are told, "Come, you who've found overwhelming joy in my Father[19], take over the kingdom we've been preparing for you since the creation of the world[20]."

Again, that doesn't mean that all Christians will be leaders of some sort when they get to heaven. That's not what Jesus and Paul were saying. But what they did say indicates that there'll be tasks suited to the gifts of each Christian up to and including significant leadership roles.

Point to Consider:
1. Seriously consider what the Bible says about Christians taking over a kingdom. In what ways does this make sense to you? In what ways does this not make sense?

---

[16] 1 Corinthians 6:2-3.
[17] Literally, "the son of man sits on his glorious throne…"
[18] Good News 30:15 (Matthew 19:28) References to thrones should be taken as references to authority, not necessarily to physical thrones. Jesus was using terminology that his disciples could understand to express something beyond their ability (or ours) to fully comprehend.
[19] Those who find God in this world are certain to find overwhelming joy in him, no matter how much they may suffer physically.
[20] Good News 40:28 (Matthew 25:34).

CHRISTIANITY 103 – HOPE—THE ULTIMATE REWARD - PART 3

THE ETERNAL CREATOR

Now, someone might ask, "What will we have authority over? After all, when we get to heaven, we'll no longer have authority on earth. Besides, even if we were to be given some sort of authority on earth, at some point the earth will be destroyed long before eternity's over. What then? How can we have authority?" One of the false pictures we have of heaven is of everybody wearing golden crowns. But if everybody's a ruler, then no one's a ruler, because there's no one to rule over. (In fact, the crowns promised to Christians in heaven should be thought of as symbolic of authority, not as golden diadems. The actual root of the word for "crown" used in the New Testament for the reward of Christians is the name of the laurel plant used to make the victor's crown given to victorious athletes or warriors—though this word was also sometimes used for golden crowns. "Diadem" was the more specific term for the golden crown. The idea of the victor's crown is appropriate because we'll have emerged victorious over sin and death.)

The passages in 1Corinthians and Matthew mentioned above certainly do imply authority, and in the Revelation we read that we'll reign for all eternity[1]. So we're back to the issue of how we can reign if there's no one to reign over?

The answer's simple, but it's one we generally don't consider. It's also important for many reasons. The answer, in simple terms, is that God's a creator. It would be arrogant to think that the infinite, all-powerful creator of the universe has created just once in all eternity, and that one creation is our own universe with us as the crowning achievement of that creation.

In this world we see that creators create. It's in their nature. True creators can't stop creating, even if they live in deep poverty in order to continue creating. I've heard that there was a time when Pablo Picasso had to burn some of his own artwork to keep from freezing to death, but he kept on painting. There's no reason to believe that the creator who created these creative people wouldn't also be a prolific creator. After all, earthly creators received their creative gifts from God. Indeed, there's every reason to believe that God has always been and always will be a prolific creator, and that his creations are practically infinite in number and variety.

Some folks reject this concept because of a human perspective. They see God's son dying on the cross, and they know that they could never willingly give one of their children to die for others—especially for enemies in rebellion. Based on this, they assume that God couldn't possibly have done this more than one time. But that view neglects the infinite love of God. Before this world was formed, God knew that he'd have to come to this world and suffer the agony of the cross[2]. Yet he considered the creation to be worth the cost. In Hebrews we read that Jesus (God in the flesh), "for the joy that he could see ahead, endured the cross, despising the shame[3]."

If God's love was strong enough to do this once, why would we conclude that it couldn't be strong enough to do it again? In fact, I believe that this is the very defining characteristic of God's love, to be willing to die for his creation. If God saw this as useful and profitable for his purposes once, how can we say that the same thing couldn't be true a second time?

So if this is a possibility, can you imagine how many different creations God may have going on? Can you imagine the variety of opportunities for service as God's agents in these creations?

Points to Consider:
1. Seriously consider the idea Christians often have of everyone having a crown in heaven. Can you see the problem with that as a reward?
2. Seriously consider the idea of God as an eternal creator. Does that idea seem reasonable to you?
3. Seriously consider what you think you might enjoy as a heavenly reward. Can you imagine God giving you a task you would really be excited to have?

---

[1] Revelation 22:5.
[2] See Ephesians 1:3-6 or 1Peter 1:17-21.
[3] Hebrews 12:2.

THE CLUE OF GOD'S AGENTS[4]

The Bible does offer clues to exactly this scenario. Throughout the Bible, God is shown as working through his agents (often called "angels" in Bible translations). The Bible indicates that these agents of God were involved in creation[5], so they were around before humans were created. But if that's true, where do these agents come from? Remember, there are both bad agents (agents of Satan sometimes called demons[6]) and good agents. I can see only three possibilities for the origin of these agents:

1. One possibility is that God created some agents as good agents and some agents as bad agents, and the bad agents will be sent to eternal condemnation along with Satan and unrepentant sinners. The problem with this idea is that it makes God (who is caring love) a pretty cruel God when it comes to the bad agents. They never had a chance to avoid eternal hell.
2. Another possibility is that God created all agents as good agents, and that some good agents rebelled against God and became bad agents. But in that view these bad agents don't have and never did have any hope of a second chance based on repentance. While this is a little less cruel than the previous possibility, it's still not consistent with what we know of our loving and merciful God.
3. The only other possibility I can see is that agents come from another creation where they encountered sin and had the opportunity to repent and be forgiven. Those who ended their rebellion moved into God's eternity to serve him, and at least some of those who didn't end the rebellion became Satan's agents with assurance of eventual eternity in hell. In other words, in this possibility, all of these agents would have experienced pretty much what we're experiencing. Actually, this is the only possibility I've come up with that's consistent with the biblical picture of God. (And this would explain the strong motivation of God's agents to lead people in God's ways.)

If this third possibility is true, it gives us important insight into what may await us in eternity. Not that all of us would serve in different creations. God gave each of us our gifts, and he knows where each of us would find the most joy in his service—and that's where he'll use us. Some may enjoy landscaping or gardening in the new world. Some may feel that nothing could be better than singing in heavenly choirs. But for the many who wouldn't be thrilled with such activities, I have no doubt that God has plans that will be thrilling for them.

An important point here is that God won't change us into something entirely different. He won't take away our ability to choose. He won't change our natural abilities (though he'll probably enhance them). He's promised to change us from mortal to immortal, but if he were to change us into something entirely different from what we are in our hearts and souls, he wouldn't be saving us or giving us eternal life—because we wouldn't be then who we are now. If changing us into something else were his plan, effectively turning us into some new and different beings, why not just create those beings and put them directly into heaven without going through the difficulties of this earth and the crucifixion of Jesus?

If this world has any meaning, it must be to prepare us for heaven. Our real purpose as Christians is to learn to live in a way that prepares us for the paradise that God's got ready for us. And a natural side effect of that effort would be that we would bring glory to God. We can be confident that the things we learn in God's service in this world will be used by God either in this world or in the eternity he's planned (or both) in ways that will bring each of us ever greater joy in his service. And because of that, we'll praise God, not because he wants us to bolster his ego, but because we won't be able to shut up about how wonderful he's made our lives.

Points to Consider:
1. Seriously consider this "clue of God's agents." Do the three choices mentioned seem to cover the possibilities? Would you agree that the third one is the only one that really makes sense?

---

[4] The word "angel" means "agent." There are actually places in the Bible where it's impossible to tell if the word should be translated to indicate a heavenly messenger or a human messenger—for example in Judges 2:1-4. The word "angel" is actually not a real translation of the biblical term—it just puts a Greek word into English letters.

[5] See Job 38:4-7 where God's speaking.

[6] See Revelation 12:9.

2. Seriously consider the concept of being assigned to work as one of God's agents. From the Bible we know that some of God's agents serve as his army; some serve to protect children; some bring messages from God; and we don't know how much more they do. Can you think of something you'd like to do if you were one of God's agents?

3. Seriously consider the idea that our purpose in this life is to learn the lessons that will prepare us for living in heaven. Does that make more sense to you than having a purpose of simply bringing glory to God? Can you see how doing this would bring more glory to God than simply trying to give glory to God without doing this?

VACATIONS IN HEAVEN

Just as there are wonderful things to do in heaven, can you imagine the vacations? First, since we'll have eternity to work with, there'll be no limit to how long our vacations can be. Have you ever gone on vacation and felt rushed from the moment you left until the moment you returned? Have you ever come back from vacation feeling that you needed a vacation from the vacation? Have you ever arrived back from vacation more stressed than when you left because of all the work that's piled up while you were on vacation? None of that will be true in heaven.

The key lesson we need to learn in this world is that God's way is about caring for others' needs. (And when we do care for the needs of others as God's team, we will bring glory to God.) Since everyone in heaven will have learned that lesson, you'll be surrounded by caring people. When you need a vacation, there'll be folks glad to take over your responsibilities while you're on vacation. And when you get back from your vacation, they'll gladly turn things over to you again as they go to help someone else, singing God's praises all the way.

While you're on vacation, there'll be others who will want your vacation to be as wonderful as it can be. Whatever would make your vacation better, someone will be there to offer just that. Whoever you meet will be glad to see you and glad to talk with you about anything.

If you want to go to the mountains and hike through the woods, you won't have anything to fear from animals or thorns or pitfalls. The colors of the world will be more brilliant than anything in this world, and the variety of the scenery will be more wonderful and beautiful than anything in this world.

If you want to go to the seashore and swim in the ocean or lie on the beach, you'll be able to do that. If you'd like to surf the waves, there'll be waves more wonderful than anything on earth. If you want to go water skiing, there'll be a large fish to pull you at whatever speed you like.

If you want to float a raft through rapids or wade out into a stream, you'll be able to do so without fear. If you want to fly, you'll be able to do that without needing wings. There'll be no limit to the wonderful experiences you can have on your vacations, but the best part will be all the wonderful people who'll be there to share the experiences. And if you do want some time alone, there'll be plenty of places to find that, whether it's a lonely beach or a high mountain or swimming to the bottom of the ocean without needing any diving gear.

And there's more, much more. Have a lion or a wolf for a pet? No problem. Help design a new world for a new creation God's planned? No problem. Whatever you can imagine, heaven will be better than that. And if what I imagine is wrong, well the only way it can be wrong given what God has told us in the Bible is that heaven is better than what I've imagined. **REJOICE IN YOUR HOPE—IT'S REALLY, REALLY GOOD!!**

No, the Bible doesn't tell us these things will be in heaven, but the Bible does tell us that what will be there is better than anything here on earth—better than anything we can imagine[7]. We can't imagine the good things God's preparing for us, but we can know that it's really, really wonderful and that heaven will be far, far better than this earth. We can be certain that any joy we find in this world will be exceeded in some way by the joys we find in heaven!

Point to Consider:
1. Seriously consider what you might like as a vacation in heaven. If you accept the message of the Bible that heaven is better than anything we can imagine (and therefore even better than what's suggested here), would you be willing to trade a few years of worldly pleasures or even of life here for an eternity of life there?

---

[7] See 1Corinthians 2:9.

UNLIMITED TASKS

Given the concept of unlimited numbers and kinds of creations, at any given time there would be limitless opportunities to serve God in one or more of his creations; just as those we call 'angels' (God's agents) serve him in our creation. We have no idea how many agents serve God in this creation, or what all they do, but from the Bible we do know that God does much of his work through these agents. In fact, this seems to be a characteristic of God, for in a similar way he works through Christians to carry out his will in this world (which could be seen as preparing us for our roles in eternity). Apparently, God finds joy in having his creations use their gifts in his service much as parents find joy in seeing their children doing tasks they approve. (And anyone who's experienced it knows that we find joy in using our gifts in his service—a true win-win situation!)

When we consider what this means to us, the news is really very good. No matter what talents we may have, no matter what interests we may have, somewhere in God's infinite creations there's certain to be a place where we can serve God by doing exactly the things that bring us the most joy. Indeed, the one who knows us much better than we know ourselves and loves us with an infinite love will be the one to assign our tasks in eternity. You may not even be able to imagine what would work for you, but God knows.

A PICTURE OF ETERNITY

Now, let's take a look at what this might mean. What follows here is just a story meant to illustrate some aspects of what we may experience in God's eternity based on what the Bible teaches.

Jim woke up in a beautiful meadow surrounded by tall trees. He opened his eyes to see the most beautiful scenery he'd ever seen. Around him, the colors of the world seemed clearer and more vibrant than anything he could ever remember seeing before. He saw colors and shades of color he couldn't remember ever seeing before.

Lying still for a moment in this park, Jim heard the sound of voices and turned to look. He saw a group of people approaching him, and before they reached him he realized that they were all his closest friends and loved ones. Leading the group he saw his grandfather who'd taught him so many wonderful things as a child. As they approached him, they were all obviously excited to see him, and they began to share what had been happening since they last saw each other.

Jim got up and started to talk and laugh with the group as they moved off together down a pathway in the park. Among other things, they were talking about his new job. He was aware that he had this exciting new job, though he didn't recall looking for it. He was already excited about it, describing to the others the things he intended to do. His mind filled with the exciting possibilities he could see, and he could already tell that there were more possibilities that he hadn't considered yet. Others in the group offered suggestions or encouragement.

Suddenly he realized—these were the loved ones he'd thought of as dead. Dimly he recalled a crisis situation just before he woke in the park. Now he was with them. Yet he couldn't bring himself to think of himself as dead. He wasn't dead. Those he once thought of as dead weren't dead. No, where he had been would more accurately be described as dead than where he and these others were now.

As they moved down the path, Jim saw a shining, beautiful city ahead, and more people came into view. Unlike cities he'd known before, this city gleamed with cleanliness and seemed somehow to radiate goodness.

Some people along the path were working in gardens of breathtaking beauty. Some were in groups talking excitedly about this or that undertaking. Some rushed by on their business, but from each one Jim could feel a powerful sense of caring love. The love was so strong; he felt he could almost float in it. He knew, beyond any doubt, that there'd be no danger here. Suddenly, the idea of a lock like he used to use so often in his earthly life came to his mind, and he couldn't restrain his laughter at the idea. There'd be no locks here.

Then someone in a group nearby broke into song. The song was clear, beautiful, and exciting. Others joined in the song. It was a song of joy in what each one was doing. Jim had never been a singer, but he found himself caught up in the song. Though he didn't sing, his soul joined in the song. What a thrill! The joy was so powerful that he could hardly contain it. How long did the song go on? Time seemed to mean nothing.

When the song shifted to a background presence, Jim asked his grandfather, "Is this heaven? If it is, when do we get to see Jesus?"

To this his grandfather replied, "When you want to see Jesus, just open your eyes and look."

Jim wondered at this answer, but when he tried, he was suddenly overwhelmed by love so powerful it seemed to shake the earth under his feet. His eyes filled with tears of joy and wonder as he saw the Lord before him, reaching to brush the tears of joy from his face and grasp him in the most wonderful hug he'd ever experienced. Among all the wonders he was experiencing, this was the most awesome. He realized that he was meeting the one who'd be his boss on his new job. It was as if waves of awe and wonder and love flowed over him. What joy! Yet in his heart, perhaps the most exciting thing Jim knew was that this was only the beginning[8].

Points to Consider:
1. Seriously consider this picture of eternity. Does this seem good? Does it seem to be consistent with what the Bible says? Does it seem to be consistent with what you know about God?
2. Thinking about this story, can you think of anything that might be different while still being this good? (There are things that might add to this.)

NO BOREDOM THERE

While this picture of eternity is, without doubt, inaccurate in some of its details, perhaps it brings home the point just a little bit—that eternity as God has planned it is exciting, thrilling, good news. There'll be no boredom in God's eternity. The Infinite Creator has more than enough to keep all of us busy at exactly the things that we'd want most to do. And when one of us begins to get even close to the point where boredom might be sensed, God will be there to say, "Come with me, my child. Others are eager to do this work. I have a new assignment for you—one that you've really wanted to do." I don't know the details of how this will work, but I'm confident that heaven will work so well and be so good that if we could catch even a glimpse of what's coming, we'd be more than eager to get there. And that's what God wants.

Just consider, if God made this world as good as it is with all the evil and corruption in it, don't you think he can do a whole lot better in a world without such evil and corruption. If God designed us to find joy in the things of this world, don't you think he knows how to do even better in what he's planned?

Point to Consider:
1. Think back to when we addressed being bored with nothing to do. How does this compare to the scenario described here? Does this seem consistent with what you know about God?

THE REST IN HEAVEN

Now, this brings up an important point. The Bible says that we'll rest from our labors in eternity[9]. Yet the ideas we've looked at here indicate that we'll have new and more challenging labors. Is this a conflict? Not really.

From God's perspective, real labor is our struggle against sin. That's the hardest part of this life for a Christian—and that's the labor that we'll leave behind. Battling sin is difficult, depressing (impossible to win), and exhausting. Working for God is thrilling, never beyond our capability, and energizing. God's reward for those who've found joy in his service is even greater joy in even greater service. That's truly heaven!

Think about this. Boredom isn't restful. When a fight that seems like it can't be won and that goes on and on is finally won, that's true rest. When a person's at peace with who he or she is and what he or she's doing, that's true rest. God offers true rest within this environment of exciting work.

Jesus said, "Come to me, all of you who work so hard and who are carrying such heavy loads, and I'll give you rest. Put on the harness to work for me and find out what it's like to serve me. You'll find that I'm gentle and humble, and you'll find the rest that really matters - rest for your souls! For the harness I'll put on you is easy to wear and the burden I'll give you to carry is light[10]." God doesn't promise us eternal boredom in a heaven with nothing to do—he promises us release from the terrible burden of sin; he promises us unending joy in his service.

---

[8] This isn't a record of some actual near-death experience. I've had no such experience, and, to the best of my knowledge, I'm not personally acquainted with anyone who has. I've read such accounts. Some seem to ring close to the truths revealed in the Bible. Others are clearly hoaxes. I wouldn't want to add to the confusion. My only reason for including this picture of eternity is to emphasize some points I know are made in the Bible in a way that may make them more understandable or real.
[9] Revelation 14:13.
[10] Good News 17:41-42 (Matthew 11:29-30).

This doesn't mean that we won't have time to relax and enjoy heaven. The biblical teaching about resting from our labors shouldn't just be limited to freedom from the battle against sin—although that will be our greatest area of relief. I fully expect to have the opportunity to wander the mountains of the new world and walk along the banks of the River of Life and rest in the shade of the Tree of Life on the shore of a sea that sparkles like diamonds. I fully expect to have wonderful times of reunion with loved ones and with giants of the faith. But while the vacations will be great, eternal vacation becomes eternal boredom, and that's not what we'll find in heaven.

Point to Consider:
1. Seriously consider the idea of our battle against sin being the real hard work. Do you find your battle against sin to be difficult? Can you imagine the relief it will be to get out of the environment of sin in this world and away from the influence of Satan trying to draw us deeper and deeper into sin?

Summary Questions:
1. Did this section help you in any way, and if so, how? Be specific.

2. What do you see as the most important point or points of this section when it comes to Christians being motivated?

3. Jot down a note or two about anything you learned new in studying this section or anything you understood better because of studying this section.

CHRISTIANITY 103 – HOPE—THE ULTIMATE REWARD - PART 4

MARRIAGE AND HEAVEN

Some Christians are worried by something else Jesus said. Jesus said that in heaven we'd neither marry nor be given in marriage[1]. Those who've experienced marriage as God intended it have found it to be among the most wonderful blessings in this world. They don't want to be separated from their spouses in eternity.

Once again, the news is good. Jesus never intended to imply that we'll be separated. That makes no sense and doesn't fit with other teachings in the Bible. Instead, the very thing we found so wonderful in marriage will become much more universal. The strong love bonds we've formed over many years must be exclusive in this life, but in heaven there'll be no reason for such bonds to be exclusive. There'll be no envy or jealousy and no reason for envy or jealousy in heaven. Instead, each person will be able to find such love with each other person. As God's children, we'll learn to love as God loves. We'll still love those who were our spouses, and I have no doubt that, at least at first, we'll have a stronger relationship with them than with others. But the barriers will be down—and we'll have no reason to resent the removal of those barriers.

Points to Consider:
1. Seriously consider the concept of building relationships with others who are not our spouses. Is your initial reaction negative? If so, why do you think that would be true?
2. There are lots of things that people say about heaven that aren't true—things that cause people to not want to go to heaven. Try to come up with some things people have told you about heaven—things that would make heaven not as good as earth and that are not in the Bible. Do you think these people could be wrong?

SINGING GOD'S PRAISES

But what about singing God's praises for all eternity? First, while the Bible does mention singing for those who reach heaven[2], there's no indication that singing will be our main activity or even a major activity. Indeed, those who serve God in eternity will be singing his praises for all eternity (perhaps vocally for some and in the spirit for others according to each one's gifts). But the primary theme of our singing won't be what God's done in some distant past, but rather what God's doing. Our singing will be the natural response of our souls to the joy of serving God in ways more wonderful than we can imagine and to the joy of experiencing God's Holy Spirit in more fullness than we could ever experience him in this world.

God isn't a narcissist in love with himself, nor does he have an inferiority complex; he's the very source of caring love for others. And it's this love that will bring the blessings of life—true life, eternal life that's really living—that'll cause us to sing for joy with tears of joy streaming down our faces. And as the tasks and the experiences of the joy God brings are eternally varying, so the songs of joy will be eternally varying.

Points to Consider:
1. Seriously consider the question of why God would want to create billions of people just to have some of them spend their time glorifying him as some Christians claim he has done. Does that seem likely to you?

THE GOOD NEWS OF GRACE

Now it's important to understand that nobody accidentally slips out of God's grace, and no amount of sin is too much for his grace to forgive as long as you still want to live for him. No one's lost just because he or she fails to live up to this life focus from time to time. Satan's more powerful than any of us, and our worldly nature is weak. On top of that, we live in a riptide of sin, and sometimes we get swept along without even realizing what's happening, or maybe we get swept along knowing very well what's happening but not knowing how to stop. God knows our weakness and Satan's strength. That's why he's provided the one and only one perfect sacrifice for sin.

The price has already been paid. Once you put your faith in God, any sin you've committed or you're going to commit has already been forgiven. There's nothing we have to do to receive forgiveness as long as the core

---

[1] See Good News 39:48 (Matthew 22:30).
[2] See Revelation 5:9; 14:3; 15:3.

focus of our life is still on being God's people. As Paul wrote to the Roman Christians, "So there's no condemnation for those who are in Christ Jesus[3]." For the Christian, "All things are lawful[4]." (God still expects us to come to him and ask forgiveness when we know we've gone against him, just as a father wants his child to ask forgiveness even though the forgiveness has already been given. Our asking forgiveness is not something God needs so much as something we need.)

If you really want to be God's person, God won't let you fail. That's God's version of predestination.

But how can you know that you're on the right track. First of all, if you're trying, it's God's job to see that you have all the support you need, and God can always be trusted to do his part—just be sure your focus is really on God. Better yet, when we learn to pray as Jesus taught, we begin to experience awesome blessings that assure us of God's love and care. (The problem with far too many prayers is that they're basically selfish and request what would obviously work against God's interests, and God won't grant such prayers. Selfish prayers are fine as long as we're really willing to let God do what he knows is best, but we need to learn to focus on unselfish prayers and prayers about spiritual matters.) Once a person masters prayer, there can be no doubt in that person's mind about the reality of his or her salvation because of the overwhelming way God responds. This is truly blessed assurance.

Points to Consider:
1. Seriously consider the idea that God's grace actually applies to our sins before we even commit them. Does that seem too generous?
2. Seriously consider what's to prevent a person from becoming a Christian and then living in an entirely worldly way. Do you see a barrier that would absolutely prevent that given what we studied about faith?
3. Seriously consider how many of our prayers are focused on either selfish or worldly interests. Do you see a problem with that from God's perspective?

IMMEDIATELY AFTER DEATH

So what happens to a Christian immediately after death? In fact, different passages in the Bible can give people different perspectives. For example, Paul told the Christians in Thessalonica,

> For the Lord himself will come from heaven with a shouted command by the voice of a commander of God's agents and by God's own trumpet call. Those who have died in Christ will actually rise first. Then we who are still alive on earth will be caught up into the clouds to meet the Lord in the air. And from that time on we'll all be with the Lord[5].

And in the New Testament there are references to Christians "falling asleep" meaning that they've died[6]. These and other passages could be understood to mean that Christians will be in some sort of waiting mode from the time they die until Christ returns again, but they don't necessarily say that.

On the other hand, Jesus told a friend and follower named Martha, "I AM the resurrection and the very essence of life. If you put your faith in me, even though you may die, you'll still be alive. In fact, anyone who's alive and who has faith in me will absolutely never die[7]."

That last sentence is a pretty powerful statement that a Christian who dies physically would actually remain alive. And later Jesus told a man dying on a cross next to him, "You can be sure of this. This very day you'll be with me in paradise[8]."

Again, this seems like very strong assurance that we won't have to wait in some limbo condition until the Lord returns. Furthermore, Jesus told a story about a wealthy man and a poor beggar named Lazarus, and in this story

---

[3] Romans 8:1.
[4] 1Corinthians 6:12 & 10:23.
[5] 1Thessalonians 4:16-17.
[6] Matthew 27:52; Acts 7:60; 1Corinthians 15:6, 18, 20.
[7] Good News 36:6-7 (John 11:25-26).
[8] Good News 49:28 (Luke 23:43).

Jesus pictures Lazarus as already rewarded and the wealthy man as already in torment[9]. Now, you might say that this is only a story, but there's no case where Jesus told a story based on a wrong concept of how things work. (And in fact, the Bible never says that this was a story as opposed to an actual account. If it was a story, it's the only story Jesus told in which the name of a participant is mentioned.) Once again, this seems to mean that those who die don't have to wait to have their eternal destiny begin, at least in some form. And the apostle Paul said that to be absent from the body was to be present with the Lord[10].

I believe both sets of passages express part of the truth, and I believe no human alive can tell the whole story of what happens between a Christian's death and the Lord's return. What I do believe is that Jesus correctly pictures what we'll experience immediately after death, but I also believe that in some way the complete fullness of the reward isn't revealed until Christ returns, just as Paul indicates. But that's just my beliefs. Like everybody else, I don't know and I'll have to wait for the real answers. But I do trust God!

The key point here from our Lord's own words is that for a Christian, death's simply a door into a wonderful eternity where we'll find peace, comfort, and joy in serving God. That's good enough. And it's interesting that the near-death accounts that seem to ring true to the Bible all picture something similar to what Jesus described— immediate peace, comfort, and joy.

Points to Consider:
1. Seriously consider the two perspectives on what happens to a Christian immediately after death. There are many variations of these two general ideas. If the end result is heaven as described here (but even better), how important do you think these differences are?
2. Seriously consider whether there might be some way for both of these perspectives to be right. Can you think of a way that Paul's words about the dead in Christ rising first could indicate rising immediately at their physical death?

THE BOTTOM LINE

In this world, we can legitimately assume that death of our bodies is inevitable. Whatever the process of dying will be for each of us, there's a limit to what we can do about it. No matter what that process is, it's better and easier with God's help. And when we have real hope for an exciting and wonderful eternity with bodies that don't age, no matter how difficult the process of dying is, there's good news in it. Remember, if God made this world good enough that we'd want to hold onto it, he can do infinitely better in a world without sin.

THE NECESSARY LINK BETWEEN FAITH AND HOPE

The eleventh chapter of the book of Hebrews is often called the "faith chapter" of the Bible because it points out many heroes of faith from the history of the Jews. But that chapter could just as appropriately be called the "hope chapter." The chapter does focus on faith and people who demonstrated faith, but in that chapter a repeated theme deals with how this faith is motivated by hope beyond this life and this world.

Too many Christians with whom I've talked argue that we shouldn't need some exciting concept of heavenly reward to support and motivate our faith. They don't have such a concept, and they even choose to reject such a concept. But this isn't what Jesus taught, and it isn't consistent with how God has designed us. If we expect people to really dedicate their lives to something, there needs to be some strong motivation. Otherwise the response is almost certain to be limited to the minimum considered necessary—often little more than lip service.

In this chapter of Hebrews we read, "But without faith it's impossible to please God, because anyone who comes to him must believe that he exists and that he rewards those who sincerely seek him[11]." Faith *should* be focused on a reward, but with just this passage we might understand the reward as earthly rather than heavenly.

However, in this chapter we also read, "For he [that is Abraham] waited for the city which has foundations, whose builder and maker is God[12]." This passage is talking about the fact that Abraham demonstrated such

---

[9] Good News 20:54-65 (Luke 16:19-31).
[10] See 2Corinthians 5:8.
[11] Hebrews 11:6.
[12] Hebrews 11:10.

powerful faith because his life was focused on something beyond this world—that is, on the hope that he understood God was promising beyond this life.

In this same chapter we read, "These [that is Abel, Enoch, Noah, Abraham, and Sarah] all died in faith, not having received the promises, but, having seen them afar off, were assured of them, embraced them, and confessed that they were strangers and pilgrims on the earth[13]." Here again we see that the focus of a strong faith is motivated by a reward beyond this earth.

And in this chapter we also read, "But now they desire a better, that is, a heavenly country. Therefore God's not ashamed to be called their God, for he's prepared a city for them[14]." Again, the focus of faith is beyond this life, in heaven. Faith is strong when it's motivated by a serious focus on the heavenly reward.

Finally we read that Moses esteemed "the reproach of Christ greater riches than the treasures in Egypt; for he looked to the reward[15]." While this passage is another that doesn't define the reward as heavenly, what's already been said in the other passages makes it clear that this is the intent.

We need to stop making excuses for a weak faith that's based on nothing but a hope to avoid hell—in other words, not based on a hope that will provide real motivation. God's intentionally provided more than enough information to motivate our faith—we just need to accept what he's telling us. To say that we don't need such a motivation for our faith is to admit that we don't have it, even though God's done everything possible to provide it. When we say that we don't need a motivation, we're telling the world that we have no motivation, and the world simply turns away.

Points to Consider:
1. Seriously consider the passages quoted from Hebrews 11. Take the time to read the whole chapter to get the context of these passages. Consider what the Bible tells us of the lives of these people. Does this actually make the case for the importance of serious hope as a motivating factor for faith?
2. Seriously consider whether this hope is really important for Christians to live the way Jesus taught. Do you think such hope is important or unimportant?

PREPARING FOR HEAVEN

As we saw earlier, the fact that there must be an option to sin once we get to heaven is real—otherwise God would be a cruel monster. He hates to lose the people who refuse to end the rebellion, but he considers that cost to be worth the price to gain those who do end the rebellion. So the most important lesson we need to learn in this life is to hate sin and its effects. That's the primary reason that we were created to live in this world. God cannot take us to heaven if we don't learn this lesson.

But this world also serves as a training ground to prepare us for heaven. God doesn't control everything we do and every experience we have—in fact, for the most part he simply lets things run their course as he pleads with us to accept his rescue plan. But God can and does use the things that happen to us as lessons to better prepare us for eternity. And for those who end the rebellion, he does promise that he'll never allow us to be tested beyond what we're able to bear[16].

When we see this world and all the good and bad in it with this perspective, the concept is motivating. Even when things are at their worst, we can be confident that God will be with us, we can be confident that God will use whatever we're experiencing for our ultimate good[17], and we can be confident that God will eventually bring us to joy beyond measure no matter how bad things may seem in this world.

The bad experiences of this world teach us how bad sin is and how much we need to learn to struggle against it. The good experiences of this world provide hints about how wonderful heaven will be without the influence of sin—far better than the best we experience here in this world.

---

[13] Hebrews 11:13.
[14] Hebrews 11:16.
[15] Hebrews 11:26.
[16] See 1Corinthians 10:13.
[17] See Romans 8:28.

This takes us back to an idea mentioned at the very beginning of this study in Christian fundamentals. In the first session there was a comment that too many people think our purpose in this world is to bring glory to God, when our real purpose in this world is to prepare ourselves for the wonderful future God wants to give us in heaven. By this point in the study, you should begin to see this as a clear and obvious truth, though accomplishing this real purpose will, in fact, bring greater glory to God than anything else we could do.

Points to Consider:
1. Seriously consider the idea that our purpose in this world is to prepare for eternity. Does that make sense to you?
2. Assume for a moment that God allows the evils of this world to continue because these are the things that will teach us how bad our rebellion really is. Would this make sense to you?
3. Assume for a moment that the good things in this world are there to give us just a hint of how good things will be in heaven. Would this make sense to you?

SUMMARY OF HOPE

In summary: God's eternity involves excitement, love, beauty, joy, responsibility, stewardship, rewarding accomplishments, and, above all, the very personal presence of the God who is love. Good news indeed! If we could really accept this on faith—if we could really understand how wonderful this is—we'd eagerly long for the day we could go to heaven. We'd rejoice over every Christian who got to go ahead of us, and we'd look forward to our turn with joyful anticipation. It really is that good!

As long as the best hope Christians have is for a heavenly reward that they'd really rather not get—at least not in the near future—Christianity will struggle with the lack of motivation that characterizes American Christians in far too many ways. If we could ever one time catch even a partial glimpse of what God actually has in store for us, we'd be eager beyond description for that reward, wanting nothing more than to prepare ourselves for that time. That's how God meant Christianity to work—an exciting race to glory and joy beyond imagination.

Remember, any or all of the details of my descriptions of heaven may be wrong, but I trust God's word that "No eye has seen, no ear has heard, no one's heart has even imagined the things that God has prepared for those who love him[18]." Once again recall Paul's words, "If in this life only we have hoped in Christ Jesus, we are, of all men, most to be pitied[19]." We need a view of heaven that causes us to really long for and focus on getting to heaven, and we need that hope to shine forth from our lives. As Peter said, "But sanctify the Lord God in your hearts, and always be ready to give a reasonable response to everyone who asks you to explain the hope instilled in you, but with meekness and reverence[20]." You can't do that if you don't have a serious hope beyond this life!

The question I'd ask each Christian is this: "Do you really have your life focused on heaven as your true hope?" If you would be motivated to serve God, you need a view of heaven that inspires you to focus on heaven. If you would communicate the gospel (a word that means "good news") to others, a concept of heaven that's truly desirable is the good news that will motivate people to truly and for their whole lives focus their lives on God.

Let's assume for the moment that you accept this, at least in its big picture perspective. (You may not agree with the details about heaven—that's not important as long as your view of heaven is truly motivating.) How would this concept change what we as Christians do? Is there something we're doing that we shouldn't be doing? Is there something we aren't doing that we should be doing? Are we allowing our traditions to work against these biblical principles of motivation, and therefore to limit our influence for the kingdom? In other words, are we letting Satan win?

Summary Questions:
1. Did this section help you in any way, and if so, how? Be specific.

---

[18] 1Corinthians 2:9.
[19] 1Corinthians 15:19.
[20] 1Peter 3:15.

2. What do you see as the most important point or points of this section when it comes to Christians being motivated?

3. Jot down a note or two about anything you learned new in studying this section or anything you understood better because of studying this section.

CONCLUSION

The conclusion is simple: Jesus is Lord, and it's far past time that we as his people acted as if we believe that. It's far past time that we took the truths of Christianity seriously and demonstrated true Christianity before the world around us. It's far past time that we made it clear that all people, whether Christian or not, are sinners justly condemned by God for rebellion and treason—the only difference being that Christians have ended the intent of rebellion and are forgiven. It's far past time that we taught saving faith as obedient faith. It's far past time that we taught a perspective of heaven that's truly motivating. It's far past time that we practiced forgiveness the way God has demonstrated it for us. It's far past time we got serious about team meetings as real training sessions and as real pep rallies. It's far past time that we got serious about discipleship.

This isn't everything, it's only a beginning. These aren't all the areas where Satan has blown us off course and where our errors have hurt our Lord's work. There's still much to learn and much to do, but this study can provide an important beginning.

APPENDIX A - LEADER'S GUIDE

To the study leader—<u>Please</u> read and understand:

This study material is meant to work in a group where people will discuss the ideas in this manual and offer their own insights and opinions. Many people have difficulty leading a discussion-type group. Here are some important points for this type teaching:

1. Without exception, the most important factor for each lesson is to start with prayer, and in that prayer it's very important to ask God to guide your study by the presence and power of his Holy Spirit. Any study of the Bible not guided by God's Holy Spirit is very likely to get off course.

2. It's also important to keep study group prayer time short and focused. You can lose people's attention with lengthy prayers, and once it's lost, it's hard to get it back. Avoid having everyone in the group offer a prayer. Extensive prayer time needs to be private time. You may want a brief quiet time where group members can focus on individual concerns for prayer. You may also want to have someone assigned to learn about and maintain a list of prayer requests for the group. Try to limit the group time spent on prayer matters to no more than 10 minutes. Prayer is absolutely vital and it is important to have a prayer time, but Satan loves to use what is good to destroy what is better, and the purpose of this gathering is discipleship training. Jesus encouraged his disciples to focus their serious prayer time in private, and he practiced what he taught.

3. Similarly, a fellowship time is important, but keep it short before the lesson. After the lesson time people should feel free to fellowship and get to know each other better. This is another area where Satan would love to use something good to destroy something better.

4. After prayer, perhaps the most important point is knowing when to be silent. For discussion questions, after stating the question you as the leader need to **<u>be absolutely silent while you count slowly to 60</u>**. This is especially true in the early lessons when people may be uncomfortable with discussion. If one person answers quickly and others seem inclined to let things go with that, you may respond briefly to the first answer, but then restate the original question and **<u>remain silent again and count slowly to 60</u>**. The truth is that most people find it very hard to deal with long silences in a group setting. In general, before your count gets to 15 someone will start talking. In most cases, once one person starts others will feel empowered to chime in, and suddenly you have discussion. (My daddy always told me it was important to know when to shut up.) If you do get to 60 with no responses, you may want to have a short silent prayer for God's Holy Spirit to move in the group before going on to another question.

5. This study can be handled either in-depth or as an overview of the materials covered. For the in-depth approach, the group can go over every question as a group, encouraging as much discussion as possible. For the overview approach, in the group meetings the leader can ask group members to identify those areas that provided new or especially interesting information and focus on these areas for discussion. With either approach, it's important to use the count-to-60 rule at least until group members get into a pattern of contributing freely.

6. It's very important that you as a leader <u>be prepared</u>. Read the material in the book before the group meets. Go over the questions. Consider how to respond to wrong answers. You are the shepherd—you want to feed the sheep without scaring them off. You are the leader. You want to build up, train, and encourage the group. You can't do that if you haven't prepared.

7. It's very important that you as a leader expect the members of the study group to read the material. If you don't demonstrate this expectation, the members will realize this and they'll stop reading the material. Under no circumstances should you as the leader read the materials to the group. Nor should you be the one providing answers to the study questions. Either you or someone in the group should provide reminders to the group members to read the material in the days before the group meets, and keep reminding them until they say that they have read the material and answered the questions. If you can use email or text messages, those would probably work best in most cases. Phone calls can also work well. Either way, it would be good to get a response from each member of the group saying that he or she has done the preparation work. Don't back

down on this one! (Announcements in the church bulletin or newsletter are practically useless, as are cards mailed to group members.)

8. **Don't "slam the door" on someone's answer**, no matter how wrong you may think that answer is unless it becomes obvious that this person is simply trying to disrupt the group. If you are not prepared to deal with the matter, simply suggest that this topic needs to be covered in greater depth in the next group meeting, and then figure out how to deal with the issue without giving the impression of "slamming the door." Bring in outside help if needed, but don't let anyone just slam the door on someone's wrong beliefs. There's a lot of false teaching out there, and many have been misled. Find a way to make it clear that these beliefs are wrong or figure out that they are right and help the group accept them.

9. It's important for the group to understand that there'll be disagreements in some cases, but we as Christians are family and we mustn't allow a disagreement over discussion items to cause division or hurt feelings. As the group continues this study, group members will probably change their views about one item or another, so at least some disagreements may be resolved just by continuing the course. Keep the focus on what's important!

10. Questions in this manual are almost all meant to support discussion. If you're not getting discussion, try to think of ways to stimulate it.

11. Encourage all members of the group to participate in answering questions. If one person constantly jumps in to give what he or she considers the "correct" answer, privately encourage that person to let others participate more in order to improve the learning experience for all group members. If one or more people never seem to speak up, consider specifically calling on them to give their thoughts on easier questions. But be careful, some people just will not feel comfortable contributing and some may take a long time to gain comfort.

12. It's important for the leader to encourage others to speak up by thanking them when they do so and by trying to see things from their viewpoint. However, if someone offers an answer that's truly wrong, as gently as possible make it clear to the group that this isn't the right answer. If possible, get the person to think through his or her answer to see if it holds up. Ask for other perspectives from the group. Perhaps carry the question over to the next session and have the study group all put in extra effort on this question. If one member continues to press for a wrong answer, then a leader may need to work with that person individually. In worst case, it may be necessary to tell a member that this study is not really appropriate for him or her. (Satan will do whatever he can to stop serious discipleship training.) It's important to hear the wrong answers in order to know where additional training is needed. Again, try to see things from the perspective of the person offering a wrong answer in order to deal with it properly.

13. For the discussion questions, although there are wrong answers for some, there's no single right answer. Encourage the group to bring up alternate viewpoints, especially if they don't necessarily agree with some point I've made in this manual. In each group meeting it's good to ask, "What did you disagree with in this section?" and "How would you see things differently after reading this section?"

14. Each group member including the leader must accept that he or she doesn't have all the right answers and that someone else's answers may be just as valid. It's important to understand that some of the answers in the book may not be the right answers. Pobody's nerfect!

15. This manual is intentionally <u>not</u> organized into lessons. I started out trying to do lessons, and there was just no way to deal with the possible variations in how much might get covered in one session. Too much depends on how much discussion takes place and how much time the group has agreed to spend on the study in each session. At each session you as the leader will need to have read ahead so that you can suggest how many sections may be covered at the next meeting. Generally you'll want group members to have studied a little more than what you expect the group to cover. If you don't complete the planned material, just carry over to the next gathering. If you finish the planned material early, have a brief prayer time and dismiss. Very few will complain about getting out early.

16. At each group meeting immediately after the lesson time, ask members to relate any cases where they've applied what the group has been studying. Encourage members to apply what they're learning—always in a form consistent with caring love.

17. If your group takes this study seriously, going through the manual may take a long time, possibly most of a year. I'd suggest that you may want to have a mini-celebration at the completion of each major section.

18. Always encourage honesty over what may be thought of as traditionally "right" answers. Many of our traditional "right" answers have been affected by Satan either to be entirely wrong or to be misused.

19. Make the setting for your study both comfortable enough for good group participation and uncomfortable enough to keep people awake. Snacks may be good, but avoid too much food or too many sweets before going over the study materials. Where possible, seating should not be so comfortable that it will be hard for group members to make notes or so uncomfortable that group members can't concentrate on the lesson. Around a table is often good, but not necessary.

20. Questions with more than one possible correct answer should be avoided if you're trying to get one specific answer. Either make the answer you're looking for very obvious or don't put it in the form of a question. Multiple possible answers are fine for discussion questions, but not when you expect a specific answer. Asking for a specific right answer that's not obvious can result in those who answer feeling like you've called them stupid when you do give your "right" answer. Just be careful not to get into that situation.

21. While some of the questions in this manual have specific right answers and some have various typical right answers, often the purpose of the question is simply a chance to discuss the topic. This may sometimes be important in order for the leader to get a feel for what the members think and what they don't know so that the leader knows what's yet to be learned.

22. At the end of each group meeting, summarize the discussions. If there were points of disagreement, try to summarize these points in a way that encourages open and generous consideration of different views. Emphasize key points of agreement.

23. Some churches may want to use this study repeatedly both for those who've not done the study and for those who want a refresher. This is the heart of basic Christianity. If we don't get the motivation factors right, we'll never be able to spread the gospel as God has ordained that we should.

GROWING THE GROUP

1. Watch for a group member who could take over the group when you're not available. When you find one, have him or her lead the group from time to time.

2. It's natural for small groups to tend to grow in attendance if the material being studied is good and the group members become friends. If your group does grow, find a way to divide the group and have someone (usually the member who's been helping you) take over as leader for one part of the group. Then find another candidate leader and repeat the process. Christianity is all about multiplying. The longer you wait to divide a group, the harder it will be to do so, and without dividing a group just naturally stops growing in almost all cases. Once a group has 12 or more members, it's OK to divide, and by 20 members it's very important to divide.

3. When you have completed the study, if it has been helpful to the group you may consider forming a new group and going over the same material. You'll have gained expertise as a leader that will be valuable, and you'll probably find new things of importance each time you go through the study. (The leader almost always learns more than the student.)

APPENDIX B - CHRISTIAN IMMERSION

IMMERSION OR BAPTISM?

Most Bible translations use the word "baptism" instead of "immersion." Why? And why does this matter at all? Some Christian groups insist that a person can't be saved without being "baptized," but in some cases, by "baptized" they do not mean immersed. Other Christian groups insist that "baptism" is relatively insignificant, and that people can certainly be saved without being "baptized." Some teach that "baptism" is important, but not necessary. Others teach that any "baptism" that isn't immersion doesn't count in God's eyes as "baptism." There's an interesting history to all of this, and there are interesting answers to these questions, but we'll focus on some rather simple points.

First, the New Testament was originally written in Greek, and to this day, Greek-speaking churches all practice immersion, because that's what the word used in the New Testament means. The word has a secondary potential implication of immersion for purposes of cleansing. Like it or not, the use of an invented word like "baptize," which sounded like the Greek word but carried no inherent meaning in non-Greek languages, was a convenience to minimize questions about church practices other than immersion. Church leaders felt that what they were doing was right, but they wanted to avoid having to constantly justify what they were doing. By converting a Greek word for use in their languages, they could provide a definition that no Greek-speaking person would have considered valid.

Second, from historical records and from archeological findings, we know that before Jesus was born the Jews had begun a practice of immersions for various reasons with two implications: 1) the cleansing of the one immersed either physically or for some spiritual reason, and 2) as a symbol of the start of a new life, a rebirth. In the earliest days of Christianity, we also know from the Bible, from historical records, and from archeology that "baptism" was some form of immersion.

Third, early Christians saw multiple symbols of importance in immersion. Because of the implication of cleansing, early Christians saw their immersion ("baptism") as a symbolic cleansing from sin[1] [Acts 22:16], though this idea in the Bible is tied to calling on the Lord. (The implication is that immersion that didn't include a turning to the Lord would have no effect other than getting wet.) Because of the submersion in water and the rising up out of the water, early Christians also saw their immersion as symbolic of entering into Christ's death, burial, and resurrection[2] [Romans 6:4]. And because of the immersion in water, early Christians saw their immersion as symbolic of being immersed into the very nature of Christ and his Holy Spirit[3] [Acts 1:5; 1Corinthians 12:13; Galatians 3:27]. Much of this symbolism is lost with the word "baptize" vs. "immerse."

So how did Christians who didn't have a Greek-speaking background wind up practicing something other than immersion? Without going into the details, for various reasons church leaders early in Christian history began practicing "baptisms" that involved first pouring water on a convert and then just sprinkling water on a convert when immersion might have been difficult for or dangerous to the convert. There were two significant errors behind the logic of these changes: 1) these leaders believed that "baptism" was sort of like a magical ritual that would remove all sins up to the time of the "baptism"; and 2) these leaders believed that infants were born having inherited the guilt of Adam's sin. These two errors caused a perceived need to "baptize" infants and people for whom immersion would be difficult or dangerous, especially in winter when the water would be very cold.

THE REAL PURPOSE OF BAPTISM

The practice that came to be known as "baptism" isn't magical. God isn't impressed by magic or rituals. There's no magic in getting dipped in water. The sacrifice of Jesus and the grace of God are what bring salvation, and God accepts a person when that person decides to serve God (faith as described above).

The best illustration I've found of what Christian immersion is all about comes from a John Wayne movie called *The Alamo*. In that movie, Colonel Travis (played by Laurence Harvey) drew a line in the dirt and challenged the men there to die with him fighting off the attacks of the Mexican army, and according to legend, all but one of the men crossed the line. That legend can't be confirmed because all who were present were dead before the legend was written down, but the concept illustrates what Christian immersion is supposed to be for a convert. It's the place where you step across the line, where you count your previous life as dead and buried, and you count yourself as born again to a new life in Christ. It's the place where you immerse yourself into the nature and purposes of Christ. It's the place where you act out physically your acceptance of God's cleansing grace.

God knew all along that we as humans need that "line in the sand" kind of experience. Missionaries report how "converts" who have not been immersed are far more likely to be hesitant about declaring their conversion publicly than those who have been immersed. Christian immersion isn't something God needs, it's something we need that God has put in place for us.

THE LORDSHIP ISSUE

The Bible never says that you can't be saved if you aren't immersed, but it does clearly make the point that you can't be saved without accepting Jesus as Lord. Ultimately, Christian immersion is a matter of lordship. If you know that the Lord wants you to be immersed, then how can you claim that he's your Lord if you intentionally refuse or put off doing what you know the Lord wants you to do? Either he's the Lord and you'll do as he asks, or he's not the Lord.

There are some who teach that people can be saved by faith without ever accepting Jesus as Lord. Jesus certainly didn't teach that, nor did any of his followers who wrote the letters and books we now have in our New Testament.

THE SIGNIFICANCE OF CHRISTIAN IMMERSION

Again, it's important to understand that getting immersed in water doesn't impress God. And the Bible provides no special formula for what should be said when a convert is immersed and no instruction as to who can immerse a convert. Christian immersion isn't about getting the ritual right or about who performs the immersion, it's about the convert turning his or her life over to God. The importance of this act has nothing to do with somehow changing God; it has everything to do with changing the convert.

THE OBVIOUS QUESTION

The obvious question for those who delay immersion or choose not to be immersed is, "Why?" What reason can there be other than a desire to do things your own way instead of God's way? And doing things your own way instead of God's way has been the path of sin from the beginning.

THE PLACE OF CHRISTIAN IMMERSION

A reasonable question is, "Where does Christian immersion fit in God's plan?" The answer is pretty simple based on what we've studied in this series of lessons. The first step is to realize that you need salvation. No one will ever be truly converted without realizing that. The next step is repentance, changing the focus of your life from yourself to God, which brings you to faith, maintaining the focus of your life on God. Once that happens, Christian immersion should be the obvious result, because at that point you've accepted Jesus as Lord and you've learned that's what he wants.

But what if you've already been immersed without accepting Jesus as Lord, or what if you've long since accepted Jesus as Lord and you consider the water sprinkled on you as an infant to be your "baptism?" That should be between you and God. If you believe that God is pleased with your decision, then simply continue to serve him with all your heart. If you ever feel uncertain about that, then do what you believe the Lord would want you to do.

AUTHOR'S NOTE - ABOUT BIBLE QUOTATIONS

All Bible quotations are my own translations unless otherwise noted. To be honest, this isn't easy for me, but it allows me to translate with a focus on the author's ideas rather than strictly on his words and to clarify some mistaken understandings as discussed elsewhere in this book. I don't claim to be a top-notch scholar in either Hebrew or Greek, so I've carefully consulted the experts wherever I had a question. My expertise is more in an understanding how God's message works and therefore what ideas the authors were seeking to communicate—and my effort has been to clarify those ideas to form the framework in which they fit from God's perspective. What I found is that the framework was always there and not that hard to find, but that human mistakes and a tendency to look at God's ways from a human perspective have all too often concealed the awesome beauty and wonder of what God is doing. I hope you as a participant in this study will find the same beauty and wonder that I've found, and that it won't take you the 70+ years it took me to see some of these things.